1/13/86

To Bridget,
   My true Friend, aide
in "the thick of it" and
actress.
   I hope someone im-
portant will some day see
your true value.

        love,
        Sal

WALK QUIETLY THROUGH THE NIGHT AND CRY SOFTLY

Burniece Avery

BALAMP PUBLISHING

Detroit, Michigan

Avery, Burniece, 1908-
  Walk quietly through the night and cry softly.

  Bibliography: p.
  Includes index.
  1. Avery, Burniece, 1908-   2. Afro-Americans—
Biography. I. Title.
E185.97.A89A35   973'.04'96073 [B]   77-2891
ISBN 0-913642-08-8

Library of Congress Catalog Card Number: LC 77-2891
Copyright © 1977 by Balamp Publishing. All rights reserved.
Printed in the United States of America

10 9 8 7 6 5 4 3 2 1

BALAMP PUBLISHING
7430 Second Boulevard
Detroit, Mich. 48202

To the little people whose struggles and heroic deeds may have gone unnoticed, and especially to Mama and Papa, I dedicate this book.

CONTENTS

CONTENTS

Lizzie Parker and a view of some of the West 8 Mile
Road Community homes in 1926

Lizzie Parker in 1966

v

PREFACE

Standing on the sidelines of life, full of apprehension, I open the door of my heart and allow it to tell you the story of our hopes and fears as we journeyed through six states seeking a home. Some of the names have been changed and others disguised, while most officials' names appear as they are or were.

Several books have aided me in my search for historical details. *Be It Ever So Tumbled* by Mervel Daines, came to my attention a number of years before it was copyrighted. I saw it as mimeographed pages and pictures stapled together, telling one side of the story about people who lived in the West Eight Mile Road community bordering on Detroit. From Daines' Book:

". . . You like it here, then?", I asked. "We *loves* it. Day aint no place like dis place." She waved her arms to take in the little house, the garden, the rambling yard. "We has a gahden — flowahs — trees — sunshine — nice neighbahs. De house is comf'table, we has enough to eat with what we cans in de summah. How cu'd it be any bettah'n dat?. . . ."

Further on in this book, one finds:

. . . In the meantime, a tract of land should be bought in a comparable area to the Eight Mile Road development, an area close to an industrial center of employment, where Negroes have already settled, and garden space is available. Here a development of small cottages would be built such as those recently constructed in Fort Wayne using salvaged materials and W.P.A. labor, and costing in the neighborhood of $1500. . . .

Unlike Daines' work which tells *about* the people who lived in the West 8 Mile Road community, the story *of* the people who lived in this community is told on the pages to follow.

Three other books were helpful to me in my quest for historical background. While in Louisville, Ky. working at the

Actor's Theatre in "The Miracle Worker", I found information in the library to support certain incidents in my story in Mable Green Condon's *History of Harlan County;* and in Elmon Middleton's *Harlan County, Kentucky.* Two days after a devastating tornado, I had an opportunity to go to Harrodsburg, Ky. In the library there, which looked like a lost leaf from a story a century ago, I found a valuable book *The Wilderness Road* by Robert Kincaid (see Bibliography & Notes section for sample quotes from each of the above).

My thanks go to the Burton Historical Library of Detroit for some valuable historical information during the 1920s about the West 8 Mile Road community. I acknowledge gratefully the help and encouragement of Hugh McCann, Louise Naughton, and Jean and Victor Pell. Special thanks also go to Mr. Meretsky of the Automobile Club of Michigan for maps of the area, and to Mr. Doyle Mainor for pictures of the walls that stand in the community. The guiding hand of Mr. Fenton Ludtke has been ever present.

Burniece Avery
Detroit, Michigan

LEAVING THE FARM

Hope is a shallow, winding river
Propelled by a force that smooths stone edges,
Sliding silently between the sinewed feet of mountains,
Plunging suddenly to great depths in bewildering confusion.
It may eddy for a hesitant moment,
Then roll on to find the sea.

The rider brushed back the low-hanging branches that whipped his face as he galloped into the clearing. He pulled hard on the reins and the mule's forefeet almost left the ground. The animal's ears flicked forward at the sight of the familiar corn crib, but the rider made no move. His eyes swept over the clearing where a tiny shanty stood a quarter mile away and his stomach knotted.

"I'm not ready to go in there," John said to himself. He gave the mule a command, nudged her flanks, and turned slowly back into the woods.

It was a few days before Christmas in 1911. The sharecroppers were settling up for the year. Some were making plans to celebrate. John Parker was not among them.

There it was — a stubborn, ageless hut squatted on a little hill, sending up smoke from its chimney like a silent signal of hope. Surrounding it was a clearing that looked like a loosely planned garden, halting at the edge of a pine thicket. Even in the Alabama twilight, it was clear that the unpainted walls of the hut had withstood many changing seasons.

Near the piazza (porch) there were tangled shrubs with ill-concealed briars that added to the look of desolation. The summer would push the large red, pink, and yellow roses out to greet the buzzing bees as the honeysuckle arbor came alive with hovering humming birds. But now it was December in the state

1

of Alabama. None of this was visible. The ground was hard and cold; the morning found ice spewed out of the ground like strange mushrooms.

Inside, Lizzie put another stick of wood on the fire. Sparks sprayed out of the chimney momentarily. She dipped a spoonful of the black-eyed peas from the pot that hung inside the fireplace and put them in a bucket lid. She called Sally, who was playing her favorite game of asking about the bright-colored pieces that made the quilt on the bed.

"Mama, who had a dress like this? It's pink and it has some blue stripes in it . . . ."

Lizzie answered that she thought it was a dress that Aunt Josephine had made, and told Sally to come and eat her supper. There was not the commanding tone of "YOU COME AND DO IT RIGHT THIS MINUTE!" so Sally continued asking about the scraps that made the pattern of the quilt.

Lizzie was playing a game herself. She was trying desperately to keep her mind off a gnawing anxiety. She knew that Sally wanted to stay up until her Daddy came home and would try to stall as long as she could. Lizzie did not want to be alone waiting for John. She wished her sister, Ada, would come.

"Well, Ada's not here — I guess I'll wrap my hair."

Lizzie found her strings, got the comb, and began parting her hair in sections and wrapping the gray strings around each section. When she finished, her head looked like it had sprouted eighteen or nineteen branches, stiffly intertwined. Her thoughts were beginning to form battle lines, and the war between her hopes and reality was raging relentlessly. She did not want to be alone.

It was getting dark. Lizzie reached for the lamp on the mantle and found a rag to clean the globe. She lighted it. The picture of the angel guiding the children across the unsteady bridge was dusted and placed back on the mantle.

This time when she called, Sally came. Lizzie washed her hands in the washpan and made her sit down to eat.

"Mama, where's your supper? . . . Where is Papa?"

Lizzie got a small wedge of cornbread and a spoonful of the peas. "He'll be along after while." They ate in silence.

2

Sally finally asked if she could go to the spring with Lizzie to get the water for the night.

"Of course you can't go, it's too cold. You'll get frost-bitten feet. It won't take me long; you just finish your supper and maybe I can find a little surprise for you." With that Lizzie went out, got the bucket off the shelf, and started down the hill to the spring.

How many children were being told they had to stay in the house because they didn't have shoes to wear? Lizzie found her thoughts were beginning to form their battle lines. She tried to turn them into a different direction . . . maybe after tonight. . . . When John gets back from "settling up" with old man Jack Williams . . . maybe. . . .

Lizzie hurried back and found Sally nodding. Oh well, nothing to do but to put her to bed . . . being alone, she knew her mind would take her to the limits of her sanity.

What could John be doing? . . . surely he wasn't trying to do the Christmas buying . . . she told him that she would go into town to do that. Men could never stretch money as far as women could.

As Lizzie was busy getting Sally ready for bed, her mind was creating a scene . . . she could hear the querulous voice of Jack Williams . . . "Darn it all, John, you folks have run up a hell of a bill. . . ." He had said that for the last two years. But not this year! She knew exactly what they had got, when it had been gotten . . . it was all written down. THREE TIMES . . . only three times, she remembered . . . one sack of flour, ten pounds of granulated sugar, and one side of bacon . . . THAT'S ALL!

They had trusted the Williamses' bookkeeping. That was a mistake. The line of "reality" forced her to recognize the fact . . . even with proof . . . who would have the nerve to dispute a white man's word about how much you got from his store?

This vexed Lizzie to such an extent that she whirled to carry Sally to the bed and almost knocked a pitcher off the dresser. Oh! Her precious water set . . . Uncle Milton's present for her wedding . . . the only really beautiful thing she had to her name. This set of twelve glasses, a water pitcher, a cream pitcher, and a sugar bowl with a cover, all heavily embossed with gold and bright bunches of lucious cherries. If anything had happened to cause her to break one of these. . . . She covered Sally and reached for the string to tighten the window shutter and gave it a few more turns around the nail.

Then she heard it . . . the clop-clop-clop of hooves on the hard clay road. She listened, hardly breathing, measuring the distance from the main road to the short turn-off into the lot. Lizzie's heart was pounding hard as she tried to interpret the way John said, "Whoa. . . ." Was he just tired? Was he angry? Disgusted? Frustrated. . . ? She suddenly knew that she had been virtually holding her breath for a year . . . twelve whole months for this moment . . . This moment . . . it HAD to be different from Christmas of last year.

It took him an eternity to unsaddle the mule, put hay in the trough, and walk in the door. He walked in, shoulders drooping, avoiding Lizzie's eyes. He slumped down in the chair that Lizzie had gotten out of, ran his hand into his pocket, and flung eleven silver dollars on the table. After a long silence that hung like a suspended blanket of doom, he said two words, "That's all."

Lizzie fought hysteria like a tigress. She wanted to run like the wind, stopping only long enough to slaughter Jack Williams and his wife, Jenny, then continue on to the edge of the world. When she could speak, she answered with two words of her own, "I'm through!"

John wanted to explain. He wanted so desperately to find the words that would describe and lay bare his very soul . . . he searched, there were no words. He felt only raw anger and rage, rage at himself for falling short of the man he wanted to be and the man Lizzie expected him to be . . . rage for the way his confidence in Jack Williams had been destroyed. He knew how deeply Lizzie's bitterness could cut . . . and winced at the thought. Maybe if he had taken his fist and given vent to the agonizing disappointment Jack Williams had given him so casually . . . maybe Lizzie would be a little more proud of him. Proud? If he had dared, he would either be in

4

jail by now or possibly dead. . . . So the silence filled the small room and pressed hard against its walls.

Ada burst through the door, her eyes dancing in happy anticipation. It took her an instant to grasp the significance of the quiet room. The change in her expression was almost grotesque. Disillusion settled on her frail body like old familiar clothes.

She asked quietly, "What's the matter?"

There was no answer. She didn't need one. She knew that she was now one of the characters in the same plot of a year ago. The only difference was that last year there had been fury; each player had spat out the venom he had felt without hesitation. Now they seemed steeped in the fumes of hopelessness.

Ada's mind leaped back to her house where her two small sons slept. She had dared to leave them alone while she ran to get their Christmas presents from Sister's and Brother John's house. She had asked him to get a few nuts, apples, and oranges for the boys, and a cap which each needed badly. She fully expected that there would be some money, for after all, she had worked side by side with the family for the entire year.

Having seen the scattered silver dollars on the table, and feeling the burden of unspoken agony, Ada began to cry softly. How hungry she had been . . . how ashamed of the patches on her clothes . . . she and Sister had made a game of the starvation they underwent . . . "Stayed away from ole Massey one more day!"

The weight of this moment . . . these unfolding facts . . . this unmistakable realization was too great. Neither of the three had been aware of the fervor and depth of their hope. Lizzie wanted to see her marriage thrive, and certainly to keep pace with that of other couples. Actually, Lizzie wanted a great deal more than just the ordinary. She wanted glass windows like Jenny Williams had in her house, beautiful curtains, nice furniture, a decent change of clothes for her family.

Ada had a greater hope because her marriage had not worked. The father of her sons was a very attractive, sought-after young man. It had been more than he could take to be loyal to any ONE woman. Ada wanted to dress well and go to

5

interesting places in the hope of finding another man who would accept the role of husband and father.

John had a philosophy that if he worked hard and treated his fellow men fairly, in due time God's blessings would be showered on him and his family.

Each in his or her own separate thoughts was keenly aware of the lack of fruition of their hopes and dreams.

Lizzie's steel grip was beginning to crack. She walked over and put her arm around her sister, as she had done so many times since the death of their parents so many years ago.

John suddenly tore out of the house before his heart exploded. He would walk in the chill air just a week before Christmas, his wife and sister-in-law weeping, his own daughter waiting another Christmas not only without toys but without shoes or warm clothes. God! How does a man prove his worth . . . show his manhood in a situation like this?

Lizzie was so irritated that her lips popped open and closed like a steel trap — no vocal sound could be heard during the long intervals as she tried to form words to convey the explosive anger she felt.

"Jenny Williams will have plenty for her Christmas . . . sitting back in her warm house. . . ."

Lizzie wanted to talk about it and give vent to her emotions, but she knew that she couldn't utter two words without stuttering and stammering so terribly that she would probably end up crying . . . and that was the last thing she wanted to do.

She opened the dresser drawer, took the *Ladies Almanac* out, and thumbed to some well-worn pages.

"Three times . . . just three times. . . . We did without . . . we sat down hungry and got up hungry . . . molasses and corn bread every day . . . heartburn and gut growling . . . and WHAT FOR?" Frustration and anger were being overshadowed by a stronger emotion, like a thunder cloud boiling over a blue sky.

Lizzie straightened her shoulders and announced, "I'm through. I have picked my last sack of cotton; I've cleared my last field. If he wants to stay, that's up to him, but I'm GONE!

"Stop crying, Ada, we'll figure out something for the kids. They're little . . . they won't mind as long as it's something new.

6

We'll have time to make a few things. A few nuts, an orange, and a stick of peppermint candy can go in the stockings."

Lizzie's mind refused to dwell on preparations for Christmas another second . . . Three times . . . and one thing each time . . . the first, a sack of flour . . . the next time, a ten-pound sack of granulated sugar (you couldn't bake a cake with brown sugar, the kind that molasses turned into) . . . the last time was a side of bacon. She was pointing at the dates in the almanac as she checked off each item. She threw the almanac down on the table.

"There's GOT to be somewhere in the world where you can get paid for honest work . . . God wouldn't make a world with everybody like Jack Williams and Jenny . . . I wouldn't stay on this place another year if he would walk in that door this minute and hand me every cent he has cheated us out of . . . even if he would give us the papers for the mules that we paid for . . . I wouldn't stay here . . . he couldn't pay me to stay here and deal with a shifty-eyed, good-for-nothing scrapings of the earth!"

Ada had stopped crying now and she blew her nose hard. "I don't blame you, Sister, I just wish I could say the same . . . I'm so sick of this place . . . don't seem no way to climb out of this rut.

"I sure thought that Brother John would've had a little money for me — we worked awful hard." Ada's voice was trembling as she went on, "I hate to think about putting that patched coat on again . . . I'll never be able to get another man to look at me . . . no clothes . . . no . . . nothing." Voicing her thoughts grew too painful, but she could not shut them off.

Ada's eyes looked down an endless path of stumbling along with two children, begging for work, settling for giving up too much just to get food and a few clothes to keep her body from freezing . . . watching her sons pattern their lives after the examples that were constantly before them, anything uplifting or inspiring being trampled into the dust of bare existence. She searched in vain to find material with which to build a fragile frame of hope to lean on in moments like this.

7

The urge to go into the "I told you so" bit edged dangerously close to Lizzie's lips, but she knew that this was no time to add the proverbial straw. Ada already knew all the arguments against her marriage that had been delivered by Sister, Brother John, and every other cousin or close friend. She had ignored them, and now she was trying to live with the consequences. Yes, she could hear them all over again whether they were actually spoken or not.

Lizzie changed the subject. "I'm going over to the Holmans' strawberry farm Monday . . . see about getting hired as a picker. I've got to get my hands on some money. I wouldn't think about leaving you here in this hole to try to make it by yourself . . . Aunt Vella could use some help with the washing and ironing she's taking in. . . ." Ada was finding something on which to build that fragile frame of hope and she grabbed it like a drowning man grabs a floating leaf.

Lizzie heard and recognized the rumbling of Ada's stomach although Ada tried to cover it with clearing her throat.

Lizzie asked, "Did you have your supper yet?"

Ada answered, "Well no, you see I was in a hurry to. . . ."

Lizzie handed her the pot of peas and looked for something in which to put part of the bread for Ada to take home. Ada's eyes betrayed her protesting. She was hungry. The little food had been given to her children before she put them to bed. All her hopes were on what she would get to bring home from Sister's house when Brother John came home from town. She took the food, gathered her old jacket tightly about the collar, and started for the door.

"I borrowed four dollars to get some shoes and that cloth to make my Easter dress and was expecting to be able to pay it back."

"Who did you . . . also borrow it from?" asked Lizzie.

"I don't think you know him. He lives in Ward. He told me I didn't have to pay it back. . . ."

"Here." Lizzie gathered four of the silver dollars and put them into Ada's hand. "You . . . also give him his money tomorrow." Ada knew that Lizzie was vexed when she heard

8

"also" — Lizzie used the word to fill the long silences when she stuttered.

"I hate to take it, Sister, but I hate worse to be beholdin' to anybody. Sister, I sure thank you; one of these days I'll be able to do something nice for you . . . I better get on back; I don't want the boys to wake up and miss me. Tell me about the job on the strawberry farm."

Lizzie promised that she would and followed Ada just outside the door to watch her on her way. As she turned back to the house she saw it for what it was . . . A shack silhouetted against a sky congested with stars.

Lizzie looked up and felt a new strength and vigor surging through her being. She felt almost aggressively happy, now that she had said out loud the things that had been in her mind for so long.

She said, "Stars, I promise you that I won't stop until I get a home of my own . . . a REAL HOME!"

The lamp burned low with a large area of the globe turned black with soot. It was useless to waste another log on the dying coals. Lizzie sat in the gathering gloom and made plans. It seemed almost incredible that this one room with its protruding two-by-fours and newspaper-plastered walls could be the only home she had known since they had come to work for the Williamses. How could she ever have been content to call this "home?" It was turning colder; the wind blew up between the cracks in the floor. A long time ago when the lumber was new and green, the planks fitted snugly together, but time had dried it out. The house was filled with crevices, and so were her dreams.

They needed pickers at the Holmans' strawberry farm and Lizzie was hired. She stayed with Aunt Vella during the week, so she could walk the three miles and reach the farm on time. John was riding for miles each day checking out any rumors about public work, road repair, anything.

Christmas had come and gone, and February brought the hint of early spring to the hills of Alabama. It also brought Mr. Jack Williams riding by, one bright morning. John went out to the road where the shining new buggy and equally shining horses waited. Mr. Williams wanted to know, "Darn it all, John, why haven't you folks started clearing the field?"

John, who was known as a kind, peaceful man, answered in a straightforward manner. "Mr. Williams, I don't think we are going to farm your land this year. I can't face another Christmas like this last one."

Mr. Williams looked surprised. "What're you talking about? What was wrong with Christmas?"

There was silence. John's mind had not healed from the wounds branded on it at the sight of his wife's face crinkling up, as her tears joined those of his sister-in-law. He kept seeing Sally searching for the doll that was not there, and how he had found her in the cotton house one day after she had cried herself to sleep.

Jack Williams was getting impatient. "Darn it all, what was the matter with Christmas? You settled up and had some money to take home as I remember."

John's anger kindled like it had been touched by the hand of a magician. "Eleven dollars for four grown people . . . for a year's work?" John was fighting to keep his voice from trembling.

"That's something else I've been meaning to speak to you about," Williams said. "It's time that kid got out into the field too".

John found himself taking rapid steps toward the buggy . . . he stopped. "She's not going to be five until June of this year. We're not going to work your land this year."

As John started to turn, Jack Williams' voice rose, "How you gonna live?" There was no answer. "Well darn it all, if that cotton ain't in the ground in the next two weeks . . . GET OFF MY LAND!" Jack Williams slapped the horses with the reins and they leaped forward in a cloud of dust.

John went straight to the lot, saddled the mule, and rode off. He did not intend to return until he had borrowed enough money to leave. He had heard that there was work in Bessemer . . . if not Bessemer, Birmingham . . . somewhere.

Spring came. The wild plum orchards tried to outdo each other. The honeysuckle grew profusely, and the roses pitched a battle with the weeds. The little house was empty and gave

10

the impression of being unspeakably lonely with its door squeaking back and forth and its window shutter flapping. It all seemed to say in a disenchanted sort of way, "what might have been."

ON THE WAY TO BESSEMER

Aunt Vella was one of those people who prided herself on finding ways out of tight spots. When Lizzie asked about bringing her few household goods and Sally into the already-crowded quarters, Aunt Vella considered it a challenge, and before you could say "Jack Williams," furniture had been rearranged to accommodate the additional members. Aunt Vella was also the kind of person who accepted reality. It would not have come as a surprise to her if John had done the same to Lizzie that Ada's husband had done to her. There were those who made it a point to inquire about "when has Lizzie gotten a letter from John?" . . . "What kind of work is he doing?" . . . "When will he be home?" . . . Aunt Vella could tell you "It's none of your durn business" in the nicest way . . . sometimes you wouldn't realize that you had been told off for quite a while.

When the letter came around the middle of April, it was only then that the relief which Lizzie felt showed how heavily the uncertainty had weighed on her. Not only was there news of how hard John had tried to find work and how he had finally gotten a job, but there was also some money in the letter.

Lizzie's next stop was the train depot. She found that it would take all the money which John had sent to get a ticket to Bessemer. She got it anyway. This was the first tangible evidence that she and Sally were really leaving.

The pace quickened. Ada came down to Aunt Vella's. She was going to pick strawberries in Lizzie's place. Sally took care of Ada's sons, Walter and Henry, while Ada worked and Lizzie rushed around to get ready to leave. A lot of time was spent trying to get someone to buy her few pieces of furniture.

Every day she walked for miles trying to interest people in the sewing machine, or the dresser, or perhaps the bed and mattress. She wanted her sheets and quilts, and she had no intention of selling her wedding present of the beautiful water set.

It was a little strange to watch the way some of the people, whom she had known for years, acted when they were convinced that she was serious about leaving. Some were genuinely concerned for her safety, while others were cool and aloof. There was all kinds of advice being given. Some said that they had heard for a fact that people who had left before had frozen to death. Others declared many had written letters to their former bosses begging to be sent for, while others had simply disappeared and were never heard from again.

Lizzie found it hard to keep a grip on her nerves. She didn't have time to sort out all the reasons, but one of the causes was not being able to sell one piece of furniture to anybody. There were those, she thought, who really wanted it and would have bought it, but they just didn't have the money. And there were those who expected her to give it to them. Well, they hadn't frightened her with their wild stories and they hadn't bought the furniture, but she was still leaving. Aunt Vella would find a place to store it until she could send for it.

Suddenly it was the last day to be spent here. Everybody kept an eye on the clock. There was no more time to spare trying to sell anything. Find boxes to pack up whatever you could. As busy as she was, Lizzie could not shake off the uneasy feeling about not having any money. But one just didn't ask to borrow money from even a dear friend when everybody knew you were leaving town.

It seemed that the children were constantly underfoot. Sally put Henry to sleep but Walter was like a little automatic image, popping up wherever Lizzie was. His little face looked so sad; Lizzie was struck by his unhappy voice . . . "Aunty, where you going?"

"Oh, Walter honey, don't look so down-hearted. Aunty is going to send for you, your mommy, and your little brother . . . now run along."

Walter didn't run along. "Aunty, please take me," he pleaded.

Lizzie's mind was running frantic races trying to be very sure that everything was done that could be done. She HAD to be on that train tonight at eight o'clock.

Walter stood all by himself and sobbed softly. Lizzie looked at him and for a moment she allowed herself to think how much she was going to miss him. She pretended not to hear him and said too cheerfully, "Run out and play, Sally is waiting for you," and she pushed him toward the door.

The crickets began their serenade in the dusky light of evening. A few friends came over to wish Lizzie a happy trip and to help carry the various boxes, bags, and suitcase to the depot.

Lizzie looked around at her few friends, fought off the twinge of sadness, and called Sally to get her sweater as she shrugged into her old black coat. At that moment, Walter melted, not making a great noise but simply allowing his heart to dissolve. "Aunty, don't go and leave me. . . ." There was too much anguish; Lizzie couldn't stand it as she looked at the heaving shoulders.

Aunt Vella wiped her eyes with her apron. "Don't cry, Honey." She bent to pick Walter up but he drew his knees up under his chin and became a tight little ball of misery. The children started to cry and the adults left sentences broken in half while they watched through misty eyes.

Ada and Lizzie looked straight into each other's eyes; their thoughts seemed transmitted. In her mind Ada agreed . . . it would be hard trying to make it with two small children . . . getting someone to take care of Henry was not easy with Sister and Sally gone . . . with Walter, too. . . .

Lizzie broke the silence, "Well, Ada?"

Ada's eyes filled but she said with a steady voice, "Since he wants to go so bad. . . ."

A sigh was heard. It was a unanimous decision by all present.

Lizzie said that they would have to hurry, wash his face, hands, and feet, and put a clean shirt on him. It might have been easier to dress an eel, but somehow a wriggling, skipping,

13

hopping, dancing Walter was ready to leave with his favorite aunt.

The bundles, boxes, and the one suitcase were finally settled on the train. The two children were awe-struck by the bright lights hanging from the ceiling of the car, the green velvet-like covering on the seats, and all the strange people with bags and coats. The people had shoes on that were new and shiny-looking. Lizzie was busy with the "write soons," the "goodbyes," and the "take care of yourself." The two sisters hugged briefly and Ada hurried out. Some things have to be done quickly or they scratch the scabs from deep wounds.

Presently Lizzie sat down, looking out of the window and waving. There was a lurch and the faces and figures began sliding past the window. They were picking up speed, the engine wailed a lonesome "farewell", and then there was nothing to see but the countryside broken here and there by the blackness of a clump of trees or the contour of distant hills.

REUNION WITH JOHN

Sally soon tired of straining to see the passing view and began to interest herself by pretending that the strangers looked like people she knew, or rather, whom her Papa and Mama knew. She couldn't see the face of the man who sat in the seat right in front of them. His head was held straight forward; his neck sort of rolled over the collar of his brown shirt. He looked from the back like he was very handsome. Walter didn't seem interested and soon climbed into Aunty's lap and began to doze.

The rhythmic clickety-clickety-clack was broken by a whine of wind and the thump that indicated the opening and the closing of the door at the end of the coach. The conductor had entered and yelled, "TICKETS." People began reaching into pockets, purses, and bags, getting their tickets ready for the conductor.

14

Lizzie found hers in the battered purse which held nothing more than a handkerchief, a piece of paper, and a stub of a pencil. The purse still looked flat and empty, and she couldn't rid herself of the apprehension about not having any money.

The conductor had worked his way to where she sat. Lizzie gave the ticket to him. His hand was extended . . . waiting. Lizzie was puzzled. The conductor punched the ticket and asked, "Where is the ticket for her?" pointing to Sally. Lizzie was mildly surprised. "She's not old enough for half fare."

The conductor looked at Lizzie, then at Sally.

"If she rides this train, she'll either have a ticket or pay the fare. . . . Where you goin'?"

"Bessemer," Lizzie answered and her mouth was as dry as dust. She didn't know what to say. What could she say? How could she prove to this strange man that Sally would be five in June . . . this was just May.

The conductor broke in on her thoughts.

"Well, this fare will take you both as far as Greensboro. I'll have to put you off there." He reached into his vest pocket, took out a large watch, and studied it for a moment. "We get into Greensboro about three o'clock in the morning."

Lizzie was getting the full impact of what the conductor was saying and the weight of it drained her of all the strength she had.

"Mister, I don't have any money . . . couldn't I send the money back to you? I'll pay you just as soon as I get to where my husband is . . . in Bessemer . . . just tell me who to send it to. Please Mister, . . . I don't know anybody in Greensboro."

"I don't make the rules," the conductor said and was moving away. "I'll have to put you off at Greensboro."

The man in the soldier's uniform who was sitting in front of Sally handed the conductor his ticket and asked in a low voice, "How much is the fare for the little girl?" The conductor hesitated, then he and the soldier spoke for a moment. The soldier began sitting sideways, reaching into his pocket. He handed the conductor some money and was given some change.

When the conductor continued to collect his fares and said nothing, the soldier turned around and tried to get Lizzie's

15

attention. Her eyes were closed; she was praying fervently.

"Lady, lady," he felt a little embarrassed to interrupt her, but he finally touched her arm. "Lady, it's all right. I paid it . . . you won't have to get off 'til you get to Bessemer."

Lizzie tried to speak, but sobs kept blocking off her voice. She was able to say, "Thank you . . . God bless you." She handed him the paper and the pencil that she had put into her purse. "Write your name and where I can send it. The first thing I do will be to send you your money."

All the while she was talking, the soldier was shaking his head. "No, no, you don't owe me anything. No, I can't give you an address . . . I'm not going home."

Lizzie continued to beg for the chance to pay him.

He said, "I've got sisters somewhere in the world. They may need a favor sometime. I just hope if they do, somebody will help them when they need it. You don't owe me a thing." He shook Lizzie's hand and turned back facing the front of the coach.

The train sped on through the night. Lizzie wiped her eyes and tried to wrap her coat around the children's bare legs to make them as comfortable as she could.

She looked upward and said, "Thank you."

The children awoke as the train ground to a stop. "All out for Bessemer," the conductor shouted. "Bessemer! Bessemer!"

The coach was filled with stale air and the noise of people excitedly getting off the train. Bags, suitcases, and boxes were shuffled and hoisted dangerously close to the heads of Walter and Sally. Lizzie discarded several plans before she found one that would enable her to both carry her luggage and also guide the children safely. This was quite an undertaking. Some passengers inevitably feel that they must make a desperate dash to get off the train before it takes them to the next station, and they rush madly to the end of the coach, banging and dragging their baggage after them. By the time Lizzie reached the door, Sally was numb. It seemed to her that the platform was at least ten feet below. Someone lifted the children down and planted them in the midst of a sea of legs and bags. They held tightly to each other's hands and tried to keep a firm

16

grip on Lizzie's coat. The engine puffed big gulps of air and sounded tired.

Then legs began coming toward all the legs that were going down the platform. There was a familiar voice. Lizzie and John were in each other's arms. Sally was pulling on his coat and yelling, "Papa!" Walter was jumping up and down and hollering, "Unka John!"

The relief and happiness of just being together was enough to last the children for quite some time, but eventually the newness of being around so many people and the noise, confusion, and rushing pace of their first city lost its awesome effect. The children were hungry and tired, and Lizzie and John were talking. The subject must have been very interesting, because they had been talking for hours. Sally sensed that it was not all "happy" talk. She was right.

John was telling Lizzie how glad he was to see her and especially how glad he was that she had made the trip on the date he had asked her to come. This was extremely important, because that man, pointing out a tall, easy-going leatherneck with a too-ready smile, that man said today was the last day this "offer" would be good. The "offer"? . . . well, let's listen to the man tell all about the "offer."

He was a well-trained auctioneer. His eyes spotted a strategic spot in the depot; he strolled over, and by the time he had said a dozen words, he was completely surrounded. . . .

"Step over here, you able-bodied men! You looking for a job that pays you some real money? You tired of walking the streets begging for work? My company needs five hundred able-bodied men. We guarantee you all the work you can handle. We need you so bad, we'll pay your way to the job . . . pay the transportation for your family, furnish you a house and food from the company store. The train leaves in a few hours. You can be there by six o'clock tomorrow evening. We don't need but 500, and more than 400 have already been hired. STEP UP! SIGN UP! PACK UP! LET'S GO!"

A line formed and started to move slowly to the table where the man and his partner were getting signatures and giving reassuring information.

Lizzie was not impressed. She almost hated herself for being so critical. She hated to see her husband's face so happy and eager. She knew how his eyes would narrow when he saw her expression.

Why? Why couldn't he detect that this was just a "pitch"? Why didn't he ask questions? . . . No, he accepted every word as gospel truth. He was ready to leave on that train . . . having had to forfeit his first full pay, even though his boss had known how necessary it was for him to leave two days before payday.

"You see, Lizzie, the company is even furnishing us a home. They say these houses were built by carpenters hired by the company . . . not some little old one-or two-room place like the one I tried to build. . . ." But by now, John's warm anticipation had suffered the frosty chill of Lizzie's insight.

Walter swung himself up on his Uncle's knee. Sally leaned back against her Papa's other knee, wanting to be as near to him as Walter.

"I'm hungry, when are we going to eat breakfast?" Sally inquired.

Walter said, "Me too."

Here was an immediate emergency . . . two hungry children and two adults with empty pockets. At this exact moment, when John was trying to justify his reasoning, he was forced to a deeper humility. Now he was angry . . . at himself and somehow at Lizzie too.

John stood up, causing Walter to slide down so fast that he almost lost his balance and stumbled forward several paces. John's concern for the boy was evident by his effort to catch him before he fell. It took some explaining to satisfy the people who had almost been sent sprawling by this maneuver. It was a bit awkward, but it served to give John time to turn his mind away from his problem just long enough to deter the acid flow of anger.

With hands jammed into his pockets, John walked briskly away. He wanted Lizzie and the children to think that he knew precisely where he was going and what he was going to do. The fact was that he hadn't the slightest notion what he was going to do. He had taken every cent of the money he had

18

to pay his room rent until yesterday. He had known it was an awful chance to take, but he had been so sure that he could draw his pay when he told them he had to leave today. He had even been prepared for them to take some of his money out, since it was two days before payday, but to hold it ALL. . . .

He started humming his favorite hymn, "On Jordan's stormy banks I stand, And cast a wishful eye . . . To Canaan's fair and happy land . . . Where my possessions lie.

> I am bound for the promised land
> I am bound for the promised land
> O who will come and go with me?
> I am bound for the promised land."

How many times he had led the hymn in Lily's Chapel during Sunday morning service, in prayer meetings, in the field while plowing or picking cotton. It gave him a feeling of hope, and right now he needed hope.

He had hummed and wandered, and now he found himself downtown. His mind had not yet produced any workable solution for his problems. Someone was calling him. His name was Richard Johnson, but everybody called him "Slim."

"Hey, Shorty, did they come?"

John hurried to assure him that they, meaning his family, had arrived that morning. The two men chatted for a minute, and then Richard said that he was on his way to pick up his wife and their bags. John stopped him, took a deep breath, and asked to borrow two dollars. Slim hesitated; he didn't know John very well . . . but . . . well, they were going away on the same train, to the same place. So he reached into his pocket and gave him the money. Men have a way of understanding each other without a lot of dialogue.

No, the men had not known each other very long. They had met in the depot. They had been in line to sign up for the job which the man had spoken of so eloquently. John had written his name and answered the few questions. He had been shaking hands with the man when Richard had asked him in a barely audible whisper, "Mind signing for me? . . . I can't write." John had been glad to oblige, if the man didn't

19

mind. After the signing, John and Richard had talked and had gotten to know a little about each other.

John hoped that Richard would not think that he was going to pester him every time he turned around, simply because of a small favor like that. As soon as the boss sent his pay, the first thing he would do would be to find Richard and pay him . . . maybe a little bonus. He had needed money many times, but never more desperately than now. He had better hurry . . . Lizzie would be wondering what had happened, and the kids would be starving by now.

Sally and Walter were hungry, but the all-night train ride and the delightful exploration of all the interesting and Mysterious places in this huge depot had tired them so much that they had curled up on a bench and had gone to sleep.

Lizzie was left to her thoughts, and she was about to examine her position . . . what progress, what relief . . . Should she refuse to go with John? If so, how could she hope to manage with the two children?

She was saved from this, however, because her attention was diverted by a commotion in the depot that was quickly getting out of hand. She couldn't make heads nor tails of what was happening, and she was trying to find out about it from various people when John rushed in. He was carrying a bag with some crackers, cheese, and two boxes of sardines.

He began by telling what he excused to himself as a "little white lie." "I went over to see if I couldn't see the superintendent about my pay. I missed him, but the clerk gave me a little advance. I was afraid we wouldn't have time to go out and eat right, so I got a little something to hold us until we could get a real meal."

The noise had grown to such a tumult that the children awoke. Oh, what a picnic! My goodness! How often did you get a chance to eat crackers and cheese and even SARDINES! The children were beside themselves. Sally was heard to say, "This is a lot better than the stuff that Mama cooks."

John, meantime, had a chance to tell Lizzie about Geetch. It was he that had caused all the disturbance. The statement

20

the man had made about "family" in his speech was not just an afterthought. John explained that it was a "must." They would not take you without your family. Lizzie wanted to know why. But by this time, the children had to get a drink and to go into the restroom and "try," so John hurried on to tell her about Geetch.

"He wanted to go the worst way and made it known that he would marry if the right woman came along. So he met a rather nice-looking woman last week and they were married. I think the trouble started when Geetch found out the woman has five daughters, ranging in age from eight to eighteen. Now he wants to back out and she won't agree to it. Look, she's got him to get in line to board the train . . . I guess she won."

The company had three special coaches for the newly hired men and their families. Lizzie wondered how many women and men felt like she felt. The crowd did not seem in very high spirits; they just sort of shuffled along, climbed on board, found a seat and sat. She felt the same way. Maybe it was because she had not rested from her ride from York to Bessemer . . . or maybe the new job seemed just too hazardous.

Boaaarrd! The train moved laboriously forward, the engine slipped, the wheels skidded, and one could hear the muffled accelerated "cha-cha-cha-cha." John said they needed more sand on the rails. Lizzie looked at him and said nothing. There is nothing to say when your whole being rebels against doing something that your heart says you must do. You MUST do it to give him a chance to follow through on a plan that HE has been responsible for. Give him a chance to prove himself right, hopefully. As the train sped along, she made up a little rhyme . . . "Hope it works . . . Hope he's right . . . Hope it works . . . Hope he's right. . . ."

The children were quiet . . . Riding a train was "old-hat", nothing to get excited about. They had seen most of these people in the depot. Frankly, they were still kind of hungry, and maybe some of the kind of food that Mama cooked would taste kind of nice after all. Sally wondered vaguely if the man with the gold buttons would come by and make Mama cry on this

21

train. Well, anyway, Papa was here, and he wouldn't let the man do anything to make her cry. Sally wondered what it would be like when they got off. She had been under the impression that they would stay in Bessemer.

TRAPPED IN EMBODIN

The company had arranged to have the three special coaches brought as far as Appalachia on the main line, where a little locomotive would take them up the hollow to the ore mines. There was a great deal of switching back and forth, and then they were pushed backward, which made the children ill. Riding backward was not easy for some of the grown-ups, either.

After a long while, the Company men who had signed the workers up came through the coach and announced, "End of the line! . . . All out." They were the only white people on board.

The occupants of the coaches straggled out looking tired, disappointed, and bewildered. They huddled beside the tracks as if they wanted to be near this one link that connected them with something familiar. Shortly, the little engine gave a squall and started to pull the empty coaches down the tracks from where they had just brought the people.

Dotted along the slope of one mountain were some gray, weatherbeaten shacks with their fronts hiked up on stilts and their rears rammed into the mountainside. Here and there, listless children sat, as gray as the shacks, pulling stringy, dirty hair back to reveal faces as dirty and gray as their surroundings. They sat and peered mutely at the motley crowd of newcomers.

"Take your pick," said one of the men in charge, waving at the shacks.

The crowd was silent and a little sullen. No one moved.

The man continued, "It's not really so bad once you get settled in. There's the Commissary right over there! we'll go over and let you sign up so you can get whatever you need for your supper tonight."

Slowly, the crowd began to move, the women and the few children up the mountain toward the shacks, the men toward the Commissary.

The stones were sharp, and Sally and Walter found it hard to keep up because every step found them flinching from pain. Lizzie went into one of the places and hurried out again. She went into the fourth one before she was convinced that they were all the same . . . same thickness of dirt over everything . . . floor, walls, table, stools . . . and the mattress was impossible.

Lizzie stood with her hands on her hips and waited for her husband. The children walked about slowly, inspecting the unfamiliar setting. The sun dropped behind the western mountain and darkness began enfolding the strangers. Sally and Walter hurried to Lizzie. Walter lifted his arms to be picked up. He was frightened way down there on the floor.

Sally groped for her mother's hand, "When are we going home, Mama?"

Lizzie was hard put to answer her child. She couldn't say, "This is home," and she couldn't say, "We're going back to Alabama."

They went out on the porch. There was enough light to discern the men climbing up from the Commissary. They were being directed by the voices of their families.

"Over here" — "No, this way" — "The next row up" — "Right down here."

Sally sang out, "Papa, here we are."

John did not come forward quickly. He was trying to decide which he could stand up to best — Lizzie's blistering description of this place and what he had gotten them into, or her cold silence. His spirit was so low that he felt completely defenseless against either form of attack.

He walked in with his small bag of food and searched until he found a lone bulb swinging from the ceiling. He turned it on and its fifteen watts shed a yellowish light over the filthy room. It was going to be the frigid, quiet treatment. John looked for a place clean enough to put the bag of food. Finding none, he handed it to Sally.

"I better get down there and bring our belongings up here. It's going to be too dark to make out anything directly."

And he was gone, glad to have a little time to himself to think . . . "I am bound for the promised land . . . ," he hummed as he stumbled down the winding path.

The next few days were waking nightmares. John went to the mines at six in the morning and returned just before dark. Lizzie washed, scrubbed, and muttered under her breath between the comings and goings of the children suffering from cuts, stubbed toes, hunger, thirst, and loneliness. Trying to get them to eat the white bread, bologna, and clear Karo syrup was the worst part of the nightmare. They kept pushing it away and asking for things like greens, tomatoes, and chicken dumplings.

All of the newly-hired men and their families were looking forward to the first pay day, but none as earnestly as John and Lizzie. John knew so little about the actual business agreements that he felt sheepish and tried to avoid answering any questions pertaining to it. For example, he did not know how much his food bill was, nor how much would be taken out for rent. He really didn't know how much he was supposed to be making as wages . . . whether they were being paid by the day or by the hour. He had no idea how the transportation was to be handled.

Geetch's wife, Richard Johnson's wife, Pinky, and Lizzie got to know each other in due time. In true woman fashion, they realized that the men had not found out nearly as much about the situation as they should have. One thing the women had in common — all had had misgivings about making the trip, for one reason or another.

The three couples grew to be friends and the men spent a great amount of time talking with John; he was the oldest of the trio and had a way of speaking and acting calmly in times of stress that the younger men respected. The men all called John "Shorty." It seemed natural, therefore, that the three angry men came bursting into John's house, all talking at once about the fact that no one had been paid, and further, that the ex-

24

planation had been so confusing that it would take a lawyer to make any sense of it.

Later, the three women got together. They had not taken the time to visit before today, although they had seen each other a few times at the Commissary.

Pinky was livid: "He didn't bring a cent home! Not a red copper cent."

Mrs. Geetch was searching Lizzie's face as she asked, "How much did your husband bring home?"

"He didn't have a dime — but you know, I've had a funny feeling about this place for a long time. You remember the first day we got here — remember the men said something about going to the Commissary and signing up so you could get food for supper? Does your husband know what he signed? Mine don't."

Lizzie waited for the woman to answer.

"Richard never said nothin' about signing — and anyway I don't think he could'a signed it," Pinky said.

"Geetch wasn't in no frame of mind to talk; I don't know what he signed or nothin' about it."

"Well," Lizzie continued, "I'd be willin' to bet they tied their pay up somehow with that paper they signed. When they came by here they was talking about what the timekeeper said, and how he kept saying something about the 'Agreement' they signed and that the Company was only taking out what they owed . . . I ain't never liked this place from the minute I laid eyes on it."

Pinky was still angry. Her temper was only slightly cooled at the knowledge that nobody was paid.

"Richard better not fool with me; when he knows anything, I'll be back in Bessemer."

"How you plannin' to get there, honey?" asked Mrs. Geetch. "I got a sneakin' suspicion ain't none of us goin' nowhere."

This payless pay day was the beginning of many talks and discussions that lasted far into the night. The men were biding their time, going to work dutifully, getting to know the bosses and the armed guards, and making plans.

Slim and Geetch did not visit John's house as frequently as they once had. They spoke to each other just briefly and casually. For three separate weeks, each family had gotten a large supply of food from the Commissary. In the evenings, Sally and Walter would sit on John's lap, and they were allowed to go to sleep and be carried to bed each night for a long time. The only thing, there was no laughing and joking.

Pinky Johnson was somewhat like a child. She was sort of plump and round with big brown eyes and long brown hair, which she wore in a braid wrapped around her head and which quite often came loose and hung like a pony's tail. The children thoroughly enjoyed her visits, even though she was moody. One minute, she would be "It" in a game of hide and seek or jump rope, and just as quickly she would be off by herself in a gloomy pouting attitude. She missed the parties and the light-hearted fun that she and Richard had been part of back in Bessemer. Richard had confided to John that some of the fellows were too easy-going with Pinky, and that he wanted to get her away from them before things got out of hand. She was attractive and she was also childish.

Mrs. Geetch was the oldest of the three women. She looked young, and it was easy to see why Geetch had been astonished when she had presented her grown daughters to him on the eve of their departure. Mrs. Geetch and Lizzie shared their concerns about keeping their families together. Mrs. Geetch confided that her oldest daughter was keeping steady company with the one black foreman, Ben Morely, and that things looked very promising for her daughter. Lizzie didn't say so, but she felt that the young man thought too highly of himself.

The almanac was consulted frequently . . . for information about a possible wedding date and about the changes of the moon, while every effort was being made to maintain a casual sameness.

THE MEN ESCAPE

The years 1912-13 saw the formation of a new party — the Progressive Party. Woodrow Wilson won the election when the Republicans split over the nomination of Taft and Teddy Roosevelt for the presidency.

However, nobody in Embodin, Virginia, seemed even slightly concerned. John and Lizzie were unaware of any events taking place in the political arena. They were obsessed with seeking a better way of life.

Even the distant rumblings of World War I did not reach the ears of the ore miners in Embodin, at least not those of John nor those of his two friends. In 1914, they were biding their time to get a daring plan in motion.

The three men walked stealthily through the familiar streets, trying to appear unhurried and leisurely to the few people whom they met. There was no moon. It was about nine o'clock. This backward place afforded no street lights, and for once the men were thankful for some of the inconveniences they had been forced to accept. They had thought once to separate and meet at the base of the mountain by the large oak, but had decided later to take their chances together.

Geetch, a hulk of a man, was still muttering profanity under his breath. The other two men said nothing. The shortest of the trio quickened his pace. He wanted to get into the mountains. He felt that Geetch was still trying to convince himself that he should make the break. This was not good, because Geetch was the only one with a gun. He and Slim were armed with sticks — heavy cudgels, enough to crack a man's skull or stun a mountain lion or bear, but still sticks, nevertheless.

"Whatcha runnin' fer, Shorty ? . . Thought we was goin' to take it easy 'til we got out o' here," Slim said.

Shorty stopped. His voice was low and tense.

"Listen, we may as well have a final understanding right now. We all talked this thing over dozens of times. We agreed on leaving the first dark night. We know what chances we are taking. Now if either one of you fellows want to go back, go ahead. I'll ask you to give me a day before you answer any questions. Geetch, your gun would come in pretty handy if I have to go alone, but one thing's sure, I'm going!"

"WHAT?" roared Geetch, "You just try leavin' me in this hell-hole."

"I'm standin' by my word. Ain't nobody turnin' yellow," Slim assured his companions. "Keep your voice down, Geetch!"

They turned. The familiar well-worn path that led to the ore mines was left behind and they began the gradual ascent up the mountain side. They had reached the mountain without incident. God alone knew what awaited them before dawn. Shorty's breath was giving out. He slowed up to rest himself. The thought of God lingered in Shorty's mind. He and his wife had prayed. They had asked God's guidance and protection. Did he have the right to ask God's assistance to escape? His thoughts wandered back over the past two years. He had left his family to find work. After several weeks of barely keeping soul and body together, accepting hand-outs and other forms of charity, he had found a job. No pay, however, for a month. Waiting for that first pay and borrowing — borrowing. He had borrowed enough to send for his wife; the kid hadn't been old enough to need a ticket. Then, the nightmare. Why had he been such a fool? Why had he listened to this suave liar who had promised so much?

". . . and not only is my company offering you a job, but we will take care of the transportation of you and your family. You will be allowed to get your food at the company's store. And THERE ARE HOMES AWAITING YOU! We only need five hundred men . . . the first five hundred to sign up will be the lucky ones. . . ."

It was the lie about "homes" that had made Shorty think seriously about going. Lies and more lies! Homes, indeed! Actually shacks stuck up on the side of one mountain facing another mountain, furnished with a rickety bed, a filthy mattress, two benches, a kitchen stove, and a table. The agent had failed to explain that everyone was forced to get food at the company's store because there was no other store. The costs of food, rent, and transportation served as a legal binder to keep you working for the company for any number of years without one penny to call your own.

Shorty swore bitterly and then laughed. He was acting like Geetch. He wondered if they dared stop now. He wondered if they dared build a fire. He wondered if they had been missed yet, and if they were missed, where the son of a - - - - - would start looking for the three missing men. Would they try to torture his wife and kid? He didn't want to think about this, but his mind pursued these possibilities relentlessly. Nobody could remember the last time anybody had tried to break away from this "slave-hold." There were rumors — some said the men had been overtaken, beaten, and made to return. Others said the men had been killed. You couldn't believe all you heard. Shorty had to break this line of thought.

"Let's rest," he announced.

"Yeah," said Slim, "Let's build a fire; it's cold up here."

Geetch wanted to know if it wouldn't be better to be cold than to have the devils spot a fire on the mountain and come after them. Nobody answered Geetch, but the men kept plugging on.

The men had forced themselves to keep going all through the night, and daylight found them near the summit. Now sheer exhaustion overtook them and they sprawled, no longer fearing the attack of wild animals. No one spoke. For some time they lay under the slanting rays of the rising sun. As they began to shift about for more comfortable positions, Richard found an old stump and sat down. He looked at John quizzically.

"You got something on your mind, Slim?" asked John. Richard took his time in answering.

"Naw . . . just thinking."

"Must of had something to do with me; you were looking at me."

"Well, I was thinking about the first time I saw you. I really hadn't paid much attention to that fellow 'til I saw you standing in line. You were the last one, and you looked like it was a matter of life and death for you to get to talk to that man. That's mainly why I came over and got in line."

John was in no mood to carry an ounce of blame.

29

"So you're blaming me for the mess we walked into down there?"

"No, but like I said, I really hadn't paid the man any attention . . ."

John interrupted Richard, and he was angry.

"If I looked like it was a matter of life or death, that's the way I felt at the time. The man didn't have any reason to lie. After all, he was saying what the company told him to say. He probably was just as surprised as anybody else to find conditions the way they were down there."   Richard disagreed.

" I believe the son-of-a-gun knows all about it. He's a part of it. Out lying . . . dragging people in to work for nothing . . . I bet that grinning ape's got a wad big enough to choke a ox."

John felt offended and repeated his statement.

"I don't think he would deliberately lie . . . why would he lie to us? I blame the company. We worked for the company, not for him."

Richard was getting out of patience with John.

"How do you know he ain't part of the company?"

"The man looked me straight in the eye and offered me a chance to get out of Alabama, and if ever a man needed to leave a state, I'm that man. I've been in four different counties and nothing's worked out for me. We needed a home . . . I've never had a real home. How long do you think I could go on rooming?"

John didn't want an answer. He was really talking to himself.

"A home . . . warm and no leaks or cracks in the floor. He promised homes . . . not just another shack."

John made a sudden move and stood up, "Come on, let's go!"

Geetch sullenly replied, "I wondered how long you guys was gonna stand around jawing."

John had his own misgivings about the agent, but he hung on to his faith in mankind tenaciously. He felt somehow if he ever acknowledged openly that he entertained any doubts or thoughts of having been taken advantage of because of his trust in people, that his whole philosophy of life, his hopes and dreams, would tumble down around his feet. So he kept much of his thinking to himself.

30

The men stretched and prepared to continue their journey. The sun had chased the early morning mist away and the campsite could be seen clearly far below.

"How in hell can a despicable place like that look so innocent?" John wondered. "I guess it goes to show. . . ."

Geetch took a fleeting glimpse.

"I don't want to see it, even from here," and he began striding to the summit to take a look at the other side of the mountain, now that it was light enough to see.

"My God! All I see is wilderness . . . I expected to see something civilized!"

Slim joined Geetch and grunted, "Uh, uh, uh."

Shorty sensed the dismay in the voices of the men.

"I'd rather have a wilderness in freedom than face any more payless pay days or watch those guards sauntering around with two guns strapped to their belts."

"O.K., Shorty," Slim answered, "That's enough . . . we're going down, wilderness or not."

The men found the mountain offered better traveling on this side. This, plus the fact it is often easier to descend than to climb, helped them make better time. They joked and laughed for the first time since beginning this treacherous undertaking. They seemed determined to keep their spirits up, and none of them brought up the things that were eating away at their hearts. John's mind was consumed with the question of how he would manage to get his family out of Embodin. Where would he find money to send for them? . . . How long would they wander in this wilderness until they were either caught by their pursuers or dropped from hunger and exhaustion?

The sun shone longer on this side of the mountain, so it was just before sunset that the three men heard, "HALT!" They looked up to find four long rifle barrels pointed directly at them. The strangers searched them thoroughly. When they found the gun that Geetch had, Geetch tried to explain to them that he had no intention of using it. They took it, examined it, and threw it away. John's thoughts leaped back to Lily's Chapel and he prayed silently.

31

WITHOUT THE MEN

"Where's Papa?" Sally had been standing in the doorway for a long time. She went over to her mother, who was preparing an early supper, and asked again, "Mama, where's Papa?"

Lizzie didn't look at Sally but kept being extremely busy. "Oh, he . . . he'll be late." Then, after a moment of reflection, "Sally, your Daddy is very busy now and he will be coming home after you are asleep and leaving before you wake up. And if anybody asks about him, just tell them to ask me. Now come on and eat. I'm going to take a little something to Walter and try to coax him to eat. He doesn't feel well."

Sally accepted the explanation without question and began munching on the tasteless food. As always, mealtime turned her mind back home. She remembered how she and Walter used to race to the henhouse when they heard the chickens cackling. . . . She could not remember when they had had eggs since coming here. The doctor had said a lot about fresh milk, eggs, and fruit when he came to see about Walter. He had said that Walter should get out in the sun, but the few sunny days had found Walter inside, not feeling like going out to play. He slept a lot or just lay in bed looking at the ceiling. He didn't even like to talk much anymore. He used to have a question about everything and then a string of endless "whys." He wasn't much fun anymore, Sally decided, and turned her attention to the awful stuff her mother had put on her plate.

Sally held her head with one hand while she scraped the food into little mounds with the other. It was during these periods of trying to force herself to swallow the food that her mind took her back to the garden where cucumbers, tomatoes, and beans had grown. Butterbeans had climbed the palings (boards) that had enclosed the garden to keep the chickens out.

The thought suddenly struck Sally that she and Walter used to run barefoot all through the garden and the yard, and the ground had felt good. But here, the stones, broken glass, and rusty tin cans kept their feet full of sores. She didn't like this place at all; now, to make things worse, she couldn't even see Papa. There had been that time when Papa had taken her with him up the mountain to that lady's house. The lady had three clocks and Papa had wanted to borrow one so that they would know when to give Walter his medicine. The lady had acted strange. Her hair was very black and came down over her face. She had parted it with her hands to be able to see. She hadn't liked the idea of letting them have one of her clocks but finally agreed to their having it during the day if they promised to return it each night. So they had carried it back up the mountain every night.

Sally enjoyed hanging on to her Dad's hand. It was so big and strong and there were large veins that she could press down and feel the slight throbbing sensation. Sometimes John would pick Sally up and carry her because her bare feet were constant victims of the rocks and rubble along the steep path.

Remembering the pleasant times spent with her father, Sally wondered what it was that was keeping him so busy that she could not see him. She decided to stay awake all night, so that no matter when he came in, she would have a chance to see him.

"Come in," Sally heard her mother say to Mrs. Geetch.

The two women talked quietly. Mrs. Geetch came every day and Sally was used to their lengthy conversations. She went on allowing her mind to wander back to happier times . . . Springtime in Alabama . . . everything pink and green . . . the wild plum orchards, one with white blossoms and the other with pink, the house about halfway between them, the wind pushing the fragrance toward it, no matter which way it blew. Later, the white blossoms would turn into yellow plums and the pink blossoms would become red plums . . . her mouth watered. . . .

"They'll make us get out," Mrs. Geetch was saying and Lizzie answered, "And that's the truth . . . unless we can pay the rent. . . ."

It was the way they said it that sliced off any further thoughts Sally may have had about the little watermelons that grew wild, called "Guinny Knots", or the funny-looking things that looked like stunted cucumbers that were called "May-Pops" — all those wonderful tasty things were plucked out of her mind by the way her mother and Mrs. Geetch sounded . . .

not exactly angry, not exactly afraid . . . a sort of mixture of both. Sally was listening intently now.

"We can't pay rent on three houses, even if we had jobs. . . ."

Lizzie interrupted, "Pinky will have to give up her house; with no kids, they won't let her keep it. . . ."

"You got visitors! Be careful . . . I'm goin' out the back!" Mrs. Geetch whispered and ran on tip-toe out the door and waited.

The two men climbed the steps to reach the porch. Lizzie waited at the door. There was no greeting.

"John didn't come to work this morning . . . yesterd'y neither."

Lizzie replied simply, "I know."

The other man asked, "Can we see him?"

"I've got a sick boy in here; you can come in if you want to. . . . It may be smallpox."

The men leaped off the flimsy porch, their guns giving them a smart slap as they landed on the ground, looking very undignified. The tallest of the pair picked his hat up, brushed it off, carefully creased it, and put it on at a rakish angle.

"Well, if he ain't back on the job tomorrow, we'll put a 'Stop Order' for food at the Commissary."

The other guard added, "If he's out a week, you'll have to get out of this house . . . Company's orders."

They walked slowly down the mountain, the sun glinting against the bullets that girded their belts.

"They gone?" Mrs. Geetch re-entered the back door. "I know they been to my house. My kids is trained. They don't answer the door for nobody if I'm not home." She took a deep breath and then, "We got to think of something . . . no use gettin' them all riled up."

Lizzie agreed but could think of nothing to do. Mrs. Geetch said she had something in mind and left.

How she did it, no one will ever know. Mrs. Geetch's new son-in-law was the only man remotely connected to this terrifying abyss over which three families were suspended, and he was a bridegroom of two weeks. But Mrs. Geetch, her four daughters, Pinky, Lizzie, Sally, and Walter moved into the

34

house with the newly-married couple. She reminded you of Aunt Vella when it came to doing the almost-impossible.

There had to be a very rigid control of everyone's conduct in the cramped, strained, unusual circumstances where mobility was diminished considerably. The children had to be fed, dishes washed, and everyone out of sight when the lord of the manor came home. After his meal, the house was to remain quiet, and the children were put to bed without disturbing him. On the few occasions when they were noisy, Mrs. Geetch's daughter would be so distressed about it that even the little ones tried hard to keep her from going to pieces.

Being fully aware that this kind of an arrangement could last only a short time, Lizzie, Mrs. Geetch, and two of her daughters spent the days looking for people who had little patches of tobacco or corn or anything else to harvest. Sometimes they were lucky and could be used for a few dollars. Mostly, they were given some kind of food because money was a rare commodity.

Lizzie found some part of each day to go to the post office in Appalachia, three miles from the ore mines in Embodin. Going every day, she got to be known. Many times the clerk would not bother to look; he would simply shake his head and say, "Nothing for Parker."

GOOD-BYE TO EMBODIN

The summer wore on. Food was very scarce. Many meals were made of boiled wild greens, such as dandelions or poke salat. Lizzie tried to make whatever they had as appetizing as she could, hoping the children would eat it. She watched helplessly as Walter grew weaker. This, while trying to refuse to think the desperate thoughts that kept forcing their way into her consciousness.

Where was John? Why didn't he write? Was he alive? Was he in jail? What would the company do to her for their so-called 'unpaid' balance owing on food, rent, and transportation? Like the Children of Israel, she sometimes wondered if it would not have been better to have remained in Egypt.

Then one day she burst into the house. "It came!! It's HERE!"

She had not one but three letters. Everyone crowded around to hear the news. Lizzie handed a letter to Pinky, who hugged it to her chest and danced around. She hadn't said much but she had wondered and worried a lot when she had not heard from Richard.

There was no letter for Mrs. Geetch and this fact had a sobering effect on the exuberance. During the slight pause that made it evident what everyone was thinking, Mrs. Geetch asked, "Aren't you going to read it so we'll know what happened?"

Lizzie began reading the letter that had "unclaimed" stamped on the envelope:

> "I pray God that nothing has happened to you and the children. We walked into an outlaw place on the other side of the mountain. But it's like heaven compared to over there. I'm going to get you out of there as soon as I get a little money together. We are building a house. We are tired of being treated like company in these stranger's homes. They are as friendly as they can be, but we will feel better in our own home even though it's just one room. You will get some money in the next few days. Please write as soon as you get this letter. I have to know how you are and what is happening. You will be surprised to know what happened to us when we first got here. Remember me in your prayers. I think about you and the children always.
>
> As ever, John"

Lizzie was beginning to see what had been going on. This letter should have reached her about two weeks after John had left with Richard and Geetch, yet it had been marked "unclaimed" and returned to Nolansburg.

The second letter urged her to answer the first letter and asked if she was in danger or if the company was making any trouble for her. The third letter. . . .

"What do the other letters say?" everybody was asking.

"Not much . . . just that I should leave immediately. He says he's afraid for us to stay here any longer. They deliberately held up the mail. He said he got the postmaster over there to write to Washington, D.C., to the Postmaster General. Applachia was given 24 hours to deliver these letters."

The unclaimed second letter was inside the third letter with the money and tickets. Lizzie was getting angry.

"Now I call that nerve. I've been to that post office every day except Sunday for I don't know how long, and that good-for-nothing postman would tell me 'Nothing for Parker,' sitting there on his broad rump . . . and all the time sending letters back marked 'unclaimed' . . . you know one thing. . . ?"

Mrs. Geetch got up. "He's right," she said, "You better get out of here. No tellin' what these money-hongry scamps will try. There's more ways to make money besides working in the mines, 'specially if you're a woman. Let's start packing."

Thus began feverish preparations to get out of Embodin. Sally jumped up and down when she was told that they were getting ready to leave on a trip to see her Daddy and she ran to share the news with Walter.

She skipped and hopped and bounced along singing, "We're leaving . . . We're going to see Papa.

The bed where Walter lay was jostled and the faint smile that had barely brushed the thin face faded, and he turned his head with the usual, "Uh-uh." Sally was annoyed with him for not being excited about going to see Papa. Oh well . . . she was too happy to puzzle over Walter; he was hard to understand these days.

Pinky, as immature as she acted at times, felt badly because Mrs. Geetch had not heard from her husband and tried to tell her so. It was awkward and Pinky didn't really know what to say.

Mrs. Geetch waved her aside, saying, "Don't feel bad, honey. He stayed longer than I expected him to stay." She laughed, "Of course, he COULDN'T go nowhere."

Then she told Pinky to get a hustle on, and confided that she was going to ask her son-in-law to drive them to Appalachia that night. "Any train leaving . . . get on it!"

Pinky took her at her word and hustled.

When Ben Morely walked in, there was not the usual scurrying of feet and the swishing of little people out of sight. Everybody was too busy and excited getting the Parkers ready to leave. Mrs. Geetch talked to her daughter guardedly, but her daughter frowned and said, "You ask him, Mama."

The truck was empty, and that meant there was no delivery to be made after dinner. Actually, Ben Morely was more of a "handyman" than a straw boss. He had been allowed to buy the truck for next to nothing. It was used for hauling any and every kind of commodity to the homes of the bosses at the ore mines. Sometimes it was whiskey, other times it was meat or a load of fresh vegetables and fruit brought in from some nearby town. This was the real reason that he had the pick-up truck at his disposal. But it served to set him apart from the other workers, and he was happy to drive it and make trips from time to time whenever he was told to do so. Keeping irregular hours could be explained by his title "Straw Boss."

Mrs. Geetch waited until he had finished his meal and then said with a broad smile, "Well, we going to have a little more room round here — now that Lizzie and Pinky and the two young'uns are leaving . . . they want to go right now, but they maybe gonna have to wait awhile. . . ."

"Wait for what?" Ben could not hide his relief at the thought of having fewer people underfoot. "She heard from her husband?"

"Yes, got the letter today . . . shame to have to wait."

"I don't have a delivery tonight . . . I might be able to . . ."

"Good! I'll tell her!" and Mrs. Geetch dashed away to tell Lizzie the news.

Just after dark, they started loading things into the truck. Lizzie was getting Walter ready and Sally saw her put a diaper on him. Somehow Sally didn't want her mother to know that she had seen the diaper . . . She walked away quietly, thinking about how very thin he was. Sally felt bad about the times when she had been angry with Walter for not joining in the games. As she thought about it, Walter had not talked much for a long time. She couldn't remember when her mother had scolded them about giggling and acting silly.

"Come on, Sally." Pinky was picking up her suitcase and she sounded like a little girl on her way to a circus.

"Your mama said you and me can ride in the back. She's going to take Walter and sit with Mr. Morely." Pinky took Sally by the hand and they hugged everybody and said, "Goodbye," climbed into the truck, and headed for Appalachia. Lizzie tried to make Walter comfortable, and her mind sped back to the night on the train leaving Alabama and she wondered.

WALTER DIES

There was a train leaving for Pineville about midnight. They would have to change there and take a train to Harlan, Kentucky, and from Harlan to Nolansburg. Midnight seemed a long time coming. It may have been childish, but Lizzie kept her eyes on whoever came into the station. Although unlikely, it was possible that the news of her leaving could have reached the wrong ears, and if so, she might be stopped and made to return to Embodin. God forbid!

They boarded the train shortly after midnight and pulled into Pineville the next morning. Lizzie, carrying Walter, and Pinky, with Sally in tow, got off and looked around at the strange town, just showing signs of wakefulness. Lizzie knew the children were hungry and, in fact, she was hungry too. They had been so busy getting ready that supper had been completely forgotten. Finding no place in the depot to get any food, Lizzie laid Walter down on a bench. She had had in mind to go out and find a restaurant near the station, but he seemed different in some way now . . . just lying there with his eyes closed. She asked Pinky if she would mind going out instead to look for a place that sold sandwiches and Pinky went after Sally, who was busy skipping back and forth counting benches.

Suddenly Lizzie examined Walter more closely, then felt for his pulse frantically. She didn't realize she was screaming.

"Oh GOD! HE'S GONE!!"

Sally came running and crying, "MAMA, Mama, what's the matter?"

Lizzie kept saying, "I tried . . . I tried. . . . If I could've got the medicine . . . If I. . . ."

The ticket agent tried to comfort her. He was visibly touched by her grief. Pinky was trying bravely to be helpful, but her face washed down with tears. Sally, crying and clinging to Lizzie, and Pinky, with a handerchief covering her face, made a very forlorn group.

The agent was a slight man with glasses; his shirt sleeves were each held up with crocheted sleeve holders. He lifted his green visor and wiped his glasses so that he could see how to write the telegram he was about to send to John. Pinky gave him as much information as she could, then took Sally out of the depot for a walk to try to calm her down.

Lizzie was just talking softly to herself as tears streamed down her face.

"Maybe I should have left him with Ada. Oh, God, I wanted to send for her . . . but I didn't have anywhere for her to come to. . . . He needed so much that I couldn't give him. If I could've got some medicine for him. . . ."

She was rocking back and forth and recalling all the disappointments. People were gathering and speaking in hushed tones . . . asking questions and looking at the strange sight — a woman moaning, crying, and talking to herself as she knelt over a very still, small form.

The agent, having sent the telegram, went over and asked the people to leave. "Only those departing on the next train will be allowed to remain in the station, and I will ask those persons to sit on the other side of the station, please. We have had an unfortunate tragedy here and the least we can do is to cooperate. Thank you."

The people began to disperse slowly. The agent made several calls on the phone and then came over to Lizzie and said, "I take it you are just passing through. I'm very sorry that you have had this trouble. You don't know anybody in Pineville, do you?" Lizzie shook her head.

"My wife is coming over to take you to the house where you can rest and have something to eat. We can make plans when your husband gets here. I want you to feel welcome, and don't

40

hesitate to ask us for help if you need it. She'll be here in a few minutes."

Sally kept insisting on going back to see about Mama. Pinky was just bringing her back when a plump woman with a bonnet tied under her chin bustled out of an old Ford car. She half ran into the depot, pushing wisps of hair back from her gray eyes. The agent met her and spoke briefly.

She came over to where Lizzie was sitting and said, "My husband told me what happened, and I can't tell you how sorry I am to hear it. I want you and your daughters to come home with me and let me fix you a bite to eat while you rest."

The agent came over and took Lizzie by the arm and, with the assistance of Pinky, helped her to her feet. As they started for the door, Lizzie looked back at the lifeless form and almost lost her ability to stand. Somehow, with the additional help of the agent's wife, they got Lizzie to the car and she climbed in.

As the agent's wife settled herself in the driver's seat, he assured Lizzie that he would take care of everything and asked her not to worry.

Then, "Oh, my goodness, you don't even know our name. My name is Newton, Jim Newton, and this is Mrs. Newton."

Pinky answered for Lizzie. "Her name is Mrs. Parker; this is her little girl, Sally. We're very good friends, but I'm not her daughter; my name is Pinky Johnson."

When Mrs. Newton reached her home, her neighbors crowded in to hear what had happened. They wanted to know what they could do. The Newtons' door swung open time and time again all Saturday afternoon, some people bringing food and some just coming to talk and try to console.

Mr. Newton finally came home and threaded his way through the congregation of neighbors. He was a rather small man and looked a little uneasy among so many people, especially not having the protection of a window to separate him from them.

He smiled and said to Lizzie, "Those people in Nolansburg are very cooperative. I mean, they sent for your husband right away. I gather he was working in the mines. He'll be getting in here tomorrow about two o'clock."

Lizzie thanked him. Something about the way she said it

prompted him to make the observation, "I bet you haven't had a chance to rest a minute since you got here, for talking and answering questions."

Lizzie gave a weak smile. "Well I AM sort of tired, but everybody has been so kind and anxious to help, I didn't have the heart to go lay down like Mrs. Newton said. If you all will excuse me?"

The neighbors started to leave while they apologized for keeping Lizzie up. They were all insisting that she go and rest now. The lady who lived next door looked out and saw her children playing with Sally.

"I know they don't want me to stop them now," she said, "So I'll keep an eye out from over to my place. I'll be back tomorrow, but if there's anything you want me to help with tonight, just holler." Mrs. Newton thanked her for bringing the pie and promised to holler if she needed her.

Turning to Lizzie, as she began putting things on the table, "Oh, a pity, can you wait to have supper, Mrs. Parker? I know how tired you must be, but if you could eat, then you could bed down for the night. I hate to ask, but you do need to keep up your strength."

Lizzie couldn't turn down such a persuasive suggestion, although she wanted so much to get by herself and to allow this awful anguish to flow out of her breaking heart. She had not been alone for an instant since it had happened and she HAD to talk to her Lord about it. But she found herself walking to the table and being gratified by the broad smile of Mr. Newton's face.

"Sit down here and help yourself." An elaborate explanation followed about who had brought which dish, and whose specialty this was, and please try a little of this and a taste of that. Lizzie minced at the food and found her mind turning back to Embodin. Here she sat at a table filled with nourishing food and Mrs. Newton was bringing more from the kitchen. Fresh vegetables, meat, fruit pies, egg custards. . . . How often Lizzie had prayed to have this kind of food for her family. And then the fact implanted itself in her mind so boldly that she could no longer ignore it, "If Walter had had food like this, he would not have died!"

She put her hand over her trembling lips, and closed her eyes. She no longer could hold back the tears. Mrs. Newton realized she had been unsuccessful in her effort to keep Lizzie's mind off that tragic scene at the depot. She put the dish of food down quietly, walked around the table, and taking Lizzie by the arm said softly, "I'll show you where to lay down; I understand."

The next day being Sunday, Mr. Newton went to church. A few neighbors popped in to inquire about the Newtons' guests and to see if there was anything they could do to make them comfortable.

Mrs. Newton prepared breakfast. Pinky, Lizzie, and Sally sat down to hot biscuits, butter, bacon and eggs, coffee and milk. Again, it was difficult for Lizzie to eat without thinking about the overwhelming difference of this table and the meals she had put on her table in Embodin. However, she ate a good amount of food for the first time since arriving in Pineville. Mrs. Newton seemed so pleased, and she sat for a long time at the breakfast table with her guests. Soon Sally became restless and asked to get down. She was given permission and wandered over to the window and admired the lace curtains. Then she became fascinated by all the things that could be seen from the window. Meanwhile, Mrs. Newton related to the women how she had lost her one and only son at the age of five. Even now, as she talked about it, her eyes became misty and her lips trembled slightly. She seemed to want Lizzie to know that her concern and that of her neighbors was genuine. Pinky listened wide-eyed and admitted that she was learning a lot about life; that it was a lot more than just parties and fun.

They were just clearing away the dishes when Mr. Newton came in from church.

"How do you feel today, Mrs. Parker?"

Lizzie was not used to white people calling her by her last name. In fact, this whole situation, being treated as special company in a white home, being helped this way, was a new experience, and it took her best to give the impression that she could take it in stride.

"Better, Mr. Newton, thank you. How was the service this morning? I'm sure Mrs. Newton had planned on going to church, . . . but we're here."

"Oh, don't go blaming yourself, I don't go every Sunday," protested Mrs. Newton. She caught her husband's eye and asked, "Did you speak to Rev. Bryant?" Before he answered, they realized that they were talking about a matter which they alone knew about, and they seemed somewhat embarrassed.

"Yes, I did, but I think we should have asked Mrs. Parker about it first." Mrs. Newton agreed.

"I didn't want to wake her before you left . . . this was our only chance so — well, what we're talking about is, we wondered if you would mind if Reverend Bryant said a few words at the funeral. We didn't think you knew any colored minister, so we thought. . . ." Lizzie could see that they were really apprehensive.

"I would be glad to have anyone you suggest to say a few words. It's very thoughtful of you and I appreciate it."

Mr. Newton cut in with, "Then it's settled. He said he would be happy to do it IF you had no objections."

They both seemed relieved. Then Mrs. Newton looked at the clock. "My heavens! It's nearly half past one!"

That was the signal for Lizzie to rush and get Sally and herself ready to go and meet the two o'clock train. Mr. Newton cranked the car, and with a great deal of noise they started for the station. Lizzie and Sally rode along in the front seat. Wherever people saw them they immediately became the center of attention. Both whites and blacks were equally unaccustomed to seeing such a combination of driver and passengers.

The train pulled in on time, and Lizzie spotted her husband stepping off the coach. His clothes did not fit him; he looked strange in them. He confided later that his boss had loaned him the suit since he had no appropriate clothes of his own.

The trio rushed together and stood, the woman weeping silently, the man trying to console her and finding it awkward.

Sally was clinging to her father's hand and saying over and over, "I'm so glad to see you, Papa."

John picked her up and was shocked at how little she weighed. He tried to be jovial, "We're going to have to put some meat on you, girl." But water was streaming down his face and he had to blow his nose a few times. The three huddled together as though, somehow, they gained strength by their closeness after a long and bewildering separation.

Mr. Newton cleared his throat and Lizzie tried to speak. Her voice kept breaking and trembling, but she managed to introduce her husband to Mr. Newton. The men grasped each other's hands. John had difficulty putting his feelings into words, and Mr. Newton simply nodded and took hold of John's elbow. The two walked away and talked briefly. Then Mr. Newton went inside the station and John came back to Lizzie and Sally.

"He is going to call a friend of his and ask him to let us pick out a cas . . . , well, if we can get Walter ready, it's possible to have the burial tomorrow and we can leave tomorrow night."

Mr. Newton hurried out and started toward the car, indicating that John and Lizzie should follow. He explained to them that his friend would meet them at the store.

The crowd which had gathered to watch the trains come in had remained to watch this unusual activity. They stood aside respectfully as the four left to get into the car. Someone in the crowd remembered Lizzie from the day before.

"That's her . . . her little boy died right in there yesterday . . . I saw it!"

Casual Sunday afternoon strollers were astonished to see two cars stop in front of Withers Sons Clothing Store. Mr. Withers got out of his car and unlocked the door. Four people got out of the car, one white and three blacks. Then Mrs. Withers got out and all of them went into the store.

This was a trying hour for both John and Lizzie, and Sally was finding it upsetting because she saw the tears on the faces of her mother and father. In fact, Mrs. Withers had come along because she had known what a difficult time this would be for all of them. Mr. Withers was explaining to someone at the door,

45

"We are not open for business. This is an emergency. These people are picking out a shroud." Then he locked the door and went behind the counter.

Lizzie said that she wanted something to fit up around Walter's neck but she did not want it to show how very small his neck was. "He's so thin." Mrs. Withers reached up and got a box with a navy blue sailor suit in it. "This little dicky could be tucked in just a little higher and give a very soft appearance; in fact, we could place it right under his chin."

They agreed that this would answer the purpose. John paid for the suit and Mr. Withers promised that they would take care of delivering the suit to the undertaker. Mr. Newton thanked him and they all departed.

Upon reaching home, Mr. Newton found the house crowded. He and his passengers had been gawked at by people all along the way. Now they were the center of attention of the neighbors who had come to welcome John and again to do whatever they could to help. This, for the blacks, was the beginning of being a novelty that would continue on into Nolansburg. They were uncomfortable but made a brave effort not to show it.

Pinky was less affected by the death than the members of the Parker family, but even she had little appetite for the feast that was spread before them. The neighbors coaxed and pleaded to get them to taste this or try a spoonful of that, trying to take their minds off their bereavement and turn their thinking in a different direction.

John was fond of talking and swapping tall tales with other men; he usually could carry on a very interesting conversation. Now, however, he said nothing beyond answering questions. The Parkers were anxious for these kind, gentle people to know how much their help was appreciated, but the wound was too deep, and there was not sufficient time to do more than just say the ordinary "thanks" which seemed so inadequate. Sally and Pinky were invited to sleep next door, while Lizzie and John remained at the Newtons'.

The burial was scheduled for late Monday afternoon. This was the best that the undertaker could do, which was remarkable, since he had just received the body on Saturday. Mr.

46

and Mrs. Newton, their neighbors, the Witherses, and Reverend Bryant came to the cemetery. The reverend spoke briefly of the uncertainties of life and the certainty of death. The new-found friends stood with bowed heads as the words "Ashes to ashes and dust to dust" were pronounced by Reverend Bryant. His prayer of benediction included a special request for strength and understanding for those directly touched by this tragedy.

The day was closing. The sun made long shadows as the unusual group of mourners expressed their sympathy by embracing and shaking hands as they walked away from the grave.

NEW FRIENDS IN NOLANSBURG

Sally and Pinky sat silently, riding along in the gathering dusk, while Lizzie and John carried on a loosely-knit conversation.

This was Sally's first train ride without Walter and the impact of his death and burial was gradually seeping through her childish mind. Although she had liked playing with the children and seeing all the wonderful things . . . all those people who had treated her so kind . . . patting her head or squeezing her shoulder, there were portions of this recent experience that Sally tried to erase. She tried not to think about the depot on the morning when they had arrived in Pineville. And the part that had happened just a while ago out on the hill, no houses or stores, just pieces of stone with writing on them. Sally tried to forget anything or anyplace that was associated with crying.

Pinky brought her thoughts back from the anticipation of seeing her husband again after months of separation. She reached over and hugged Sally and gently brought the child's head to rest on her lap. Pinky didn't want Sally to ask her anything about the death or the funeral. "The price you paid for friendship," she thought to herself. Sally, aware of Pinky's withdrawal, refrained from talking and drifted off to sleep.

After discarding all but one passenger coach and coupling on a half dozen coal hoppers, the train terminated its trip at Nolansburg, Kentucky. The postmaster, the superintendent, and the driver of the mule train were waiting to welcome John and the newcomers. Suddenly it sounded as if they had been transplanted to a foreign country. John chatted easily, exchanging jokes with the men, but he had to act as interpreter for Lizzie and Pinkie. There was a mixture of pride and concern in John's voice as he explained to Lizzie what the men were saying and at the same time tried to avoid embarrassment to his friends. The inability to comprehend the spoken word did not, in any way, limit the genuine welcome extended to the women. With a great amount of activity they were readied for the trip to the "house."

They rode in the small coal cars behind a sturdy mule. The tracks, wooden pieces of four-by-eights, ran from the coal mine to the railroad, about a mile distance. John explained that the miners would fill a car, tag it, and signal the driver, who in turn took the loaded cars — sometimes as many as five or six — and drove them out to the tipple where they were dumped into the waiting freight cars in the siding. The tags identified each miner's tonnage and determined his pay.

"Here, if you work, you get paid," John said proudly.

When Lizzie saw the "house," her stomach tightened and her throat dried. She knew that John was watching her and she made a tremendous effort to hide her feelings.

"You know I told you it was just one room," John's voice was slightly pleading.

"It's all right — it's fine," Lizzie said, while her mind ticked off the weeks before cold weather was expected. "How in heaven's name can we keep warm?" she was thinking. She saw no chimney . . . therefore, no fire-place . . . no stove. . . .

John was busy getting the bags out of the coal cars and thanking the driver. He offered the driver pay. It was refused with a statement that Lizzie couldn't understand. The men laughed, waved, and the driver went on toward the mine.

If Lizzie was disappointed, Pinky was desolate. Had there

48

been means, she probably would have run away even without seeing Richard.

John changed into his grimy overalls, picked up his cap, filled his miner's lamp with carbide, and was on his way to the mines. Lizzie had not noticed what he was doing.

"Where are you going? You should eat something. . . ."

"It's only a short way from here and I can get a lot of digging done before quitting time." Lizzie was about to protest.

"I'll get a sandwich from one of the men," he called back and disappeared around the side of the mountain.

John was anxious to show his appreciation for having been allowed to go to Pineville and for the clothes he borrowed. He was also anxious to get away from Lizzie's scrutiny of the "house" he had brought her to.

"Miss Lizzie, what kind of place is this?" Pinky asked tearfully. Lizzie faced the question squarely, "What kind of place is this indeed?"

Here, about twenty-five feet from the coal train tracks, was their new home . . . all of ten by ten feet . . . logs notched and fitted at each corner and planks nailed in the spaces between the logs. The floor boards were curling and straining against the few nails that still held them to the logs that served as a foundation. The door hung lop-sided and scraped the floor, opening reluctantly to disclose three bunks attached to each of the three walls, leaving the front area for the door.

For a fleeting moment, Lizzie wanted to sit down and cry . . . cry for all the heartache that had pursued her doggedly for years. She didn't want Sally to see her crying . . . Where was Sally?

"Sally! Sally!! Come here! Where are you?" Lizzie was running and calling frantically.

"Here I am, Mama." Sally had gone behind the little house and found a tiny stream laughing its sparkling way down the mountain.

"I didn't see any fish in it, Mama, but doesn't it make a pretty sound?"

Lizzie was so relieved, she forgot about crying and scolded Sally for wandering away. "Don't do it again! Maybe there are snakes . . . Come on in, we are all going to rest for awhile." Lizzie hoisted Sally up on the bunk that was nailed to the east wall.

"Will you lay down with me, Mama? Don't go to sleep and leave me," wailed Sally. Pinky hesitated, shrugged dejectedly, and flung herself on the bunk on the west wall. The three tired travelers were soon sleeping soundly. They were physically exhausted and spiritually weary.

Sally woke to the noise of many strange voices. The coal train had stopped and its ten or twelve passengers were scrambling out to be introduced to Lizzie and Pinky. All of them were covered with black coal dust, the only difference between them being their varying heights and the color of their eyes. Richard ran and picked Pinky up and swung her around. Introductions were made amid a lot of back-slapping and joking. John was assuring one of the men, "We'll be there . . . no doubt about it. I left in such a hurry, I didn't lay in anything to cook."

So on the very first day in Nolansburg, the "red carpet" treatment was being continued for the black families.

John took a large can that had once held fifty pounds of lard and filled it from the stream that Sally had discovered. After building a fire outside where rocks had been placed to accommodate a pot or skillet, he placed it on the fire. Soon he was ready for his bath. The process was repeated by Richard. Each man had the privacy of the whole house for bathing. The rest occupied themselves with preparing the evening meal or just watching the mountain shadows creep closer and finally engulf the little hut in a prelude to night.

The shock of the lack of bare necessities had worn off sufficiently to allow Lizzie and Pinky to be genuinely glad to be together with their husbands again. This was evidenced by a great deal of laughter and lighthearted banter as they prepared to go to dinner as guests in their new neighbor's home.

As John closed the door, he snapped his fingers; his eyes went to Richard's middle, "You forgot yours too." John went inside again. When he came out, he was busy buckling a holster around his waist.

50

"What is that, Papa?" Sally asked, wide-eyed. Lizzie wanted to know, "What's that for?" Pinky asked Richard if he had one and if he did, why.

"Nah, I lost it," then, after a pause, Richard went on, "When we first got here, they explained to us that every man had to carry a gun. Seeing as how we didn't have any, they gave each of us one and told us to wear them everywhere we went, but I hate guns. There's no sheriff here and you're s'posed to look out for yourself and your family."

Lizzie and Pinky exchanged glances, but said nothing.

John chuckled as he led the way down the little path that ran beside the coal train track. "When we came down that mountain and looked in the barrels of four shotguns, I'm here to tell you I was scared. They searched us and found the gun that Geetch had. I think it was Bill Huston who said it was rusty and wouldn't shoot and wasn't worth a d---! Then his dad told him to throw it away. He said that a thing like that could get us killed. One of the fellows asked us what brought us to Kentucky . . . they didn't want to know anything about us except why we came. They were not interested in our names or where we had been. We told them we were looking for work. They sort of squinted at us for a minute."

" 'Well, if you really want to work, there's plenty of work here in the coal mine,' Huston said and then invited us to his house for a hot meal."

"Oooh, I bet you all were glad it turned out like that instead of being marched off to jail."

"I bet you were scared, too, Richard . . ."

"Sure, I was scared."

"Why didn't they want to know your name?"

"A man can lie about his name," Richard answered and his eyes swept the sides of the mountains, "I think there are a few escaped convicts around here."

They came to a wider clearing, and just ahead was the Rainey family standing on the porch of a sturdily-built house. Dave Rainey came to meet the guests, with the children following timidly as Mrs. Rainey rushed back into the house. Sally took a firmer grip on Lizzie's hand. Although the shyness of the children was most evident, it was more readily overcome. They did not suffer the same awkward stiffness of getting adjusted that the adults went through. By the time the children were called in to eat after the grown-ups had finished, they were already drawing straws to decide who would sit beside Sally at the table.

In the course of the evening, Lizzie learned that the swing on the porch as well as every stick of furniture in the house was handmade. She felt much better about the pitiful shelter that she had been asked to accept as "home" when Mrs. Rainey described how she and her husband had started out. Judging from what Mrs. Rainey said, the little hut was typical of Kentucky dwellings in this part of the state. The Raineys had saved enough money to get a store-bought cook stove last year. Until then, she had progressed from outside to the fire place for preparation of meals.

It was a little easier to understand each other after the newcomers had asked "What did you say?" many, many times. There were numerous "a's" sandwiched between words, and there were also the inflections. If orchestrated, they would have stretched an octave in range. The sentences, whether declarative or interrogative, were left suspended in the air.

"I tol' Jed ter fetch me a poke of them salad greens fer supper; m' backs a beena killin' me fer the las' few days and h'it h'aint a mite better," Mrs. Rainey explained.

The newcomers learned that "fetch" meant "bring," "poke" was "bag" or "sack," "spile" meant "spoil" and "lickin'" meant "whipping." Their vocabulary would have to be extensive if communication with the neighbors here in Nolansburg was to be accomplished.

Finally the guests were at the door, thanking the Raineys again for a wonderful meal.

"We was obliged to have ya'."

"It's a long time since I had biscuits," Richard added, "and that fish . . . ," his broad smile spoke more eloquently than he could.

"The young'uns 'ud a had to fetch h'it to yer, if yer had na'

52

come to get it. Ya' cain't keep nothin'; h'it spiles," Dave Rainey said.

Mrs. Rainey turned down any help from Lizzie or Pinky to clear the table. "That's the young'uns part of the work. Oh, the Hardys wants ya' tomorrow! She tol' me to be sure to tell ya'. They'll send one of the boys for ya'."

John looked at Lizzie and Pinky at Richard. The couples wanted time to themselves, but working during the day and visiting every night was not going to permit it.

Mr. Rainey continued, "We all talked it over. It'll be a while afore ya get settled and the neighbors want to help . . . anyways, it's been a coon's age since we had anybody new in the valley . . . if ya don't go, they'll blame us. They'll think we're tryin' to hog ya'."

"Well now, that's mighty nice of the Hardys," John's smile refused awareness of the lack of enthusiasm shown on the faces of the other guests. "We'll be ready!"

As invitations were accepted from neighbor to neighbor, Pinky and Lizzie learned to make do and adjust to the outdoor facilities as they plied their culinary arts.

RICHARD'S BLUNDER

The first weeks were spent trying to find ways to make the living conditions more bearable. Lizzie found courage to write to Ada, telling her about Walter's death and explaining the present situation.

One day it rained, and the frail shelter gave way to the steady downpour. Being inside was very little different from being outside.

"Shorty, you ought'a let the fellers know your plans. We can have you a four room house up in three to four days at the most; just give the word." Rainey's voice was earnest as he sized up the incompetent patch work on the shanty. "Now's the best time; saps down, timber is easy to handle, and it's a few weeks before the huntin' fever sets in."

John kept his eyes averted and hedged, "I'll let you know before long." Rainey shrugged and the coal cars moved on down the track.

Actually, John had not yet come to an understanding with Lizzie about any permanent plans. There were areas of agreement and areas of "wait and see." He knew that she liked the friendliness of the people and the money he was able to make for the first time in his life. But beyond that . . . neither of them liked the fact that there were no schools and no expressed interest in getting one. They both missed going to church. And they were waiting to see what Richard and Pinky planned to do. The arrangement of sharing the shelter had not worked out well. Obviously it was too small, but the Johnsons were making no move to seek anything else. Possibly, Richard felt that is was equally John's family's responsibility to move out. Meantime, Lizzie and John feared that if they consented to have a shingling party and to allow the neighbors to build a new house, Richard and Pinky may feel inclined to occupy it also.

John did not want to lose Richard's friendship, if for no other reason than they were the only two black men in Nolansburg. Cramped living quarters had caused all sorts of attitudes to surface, some of which were most undesirable. But nothing, however distasteful, could make John forget the time Richard had helped him when he had needed it so desperately.

Lately, there had been an unending argument raging between Pinky and Richard that was highly seasoned with jealousy, insinuations, and high tempers. Lizzie and John found themselves taking frequent walks to avoid being spectators and to allow a cooling-off period for the Johnsons. Of course, the Parkers had spirited sessions of conflict, too, and then it became necessary for the Johnsons to take a stroll.

Suddenly, the hunting season descended on Nolansburg. The betting jumped into high gear. There were wagers on who would bring in the most game, the largest game, and the rarest game. John and Richard were not in the running; they were patching the little one-room shelter and trying to get it ready for winter. It was while Richard was trying to fasten a large piece of tin to the roof that he hammered his thumb. The air turned blue with expletives as he came down to nurse his injured hand.

"Haven't heard words like that since Geetch left," John said.

"Wonder whatever happened to him . . . he sure meant to be absent when the women came from Virginia . . . just in case," Richard said remembering Geetch's hurried departure.

"Take a god to tell where he made his last track," John answered, jumping down to take a breather.

Richard's eyes swept the humps of the mountains. He seemed to be thinking about his next remark. When he looked like this, it made John wonder if the mountains somehow made Richard feel hemmed in.

"You know, maybe I should'a gone with Geetch. Pinky — well, she ain't never gonna grow into a woman. A man needs a woman, not a pouting kid." John did not want to discuss Richard's affairs and started back up to finish repairing the space by the make-shift chimney. Richard was persistent.

"Do you know, I found a note she wrote to Huston. I don't know what she was sayin' — I can't read, you know. . . ."

"How do you know the note was written to Huston?" John asked.

"I made her tell me, but I don't believe she wrote what she said she wrote. I got it right here — I want you to read it. . . ."

"Now, Slim, why don't you let it be. It's not gonna help for me to read it. Tear it up and forget it."

Richard was holding out a crumpled paper. "I want to know what she's saying to that blue-eyed son of a -----."

The picturesque discription was interrupted by the sound of Sally's squealing laughter as she ran up the path followed closely by Pinky. They were racing to see who would get to the door first. Pinky allowed Sally to win by a half step and they kept on around the back and down the incline to the stream to cool their bare feet. Richard stuffed the paper into his pocket and went back up the ladder.

"Where's the berries for that pie?" John asked, not really caring because of his overwhelming relief at being saved from reading the note.

"Somebody else found Mrs. Rainey's secret patch; it was clean," Lizzie said, sitting on a stump fanning with her apron. "How you makin' out with the work?" She got up and started to circle the little hut inspecting as she went. "It's gonna turn cold pretty soon; when you gonna bring the stove from the Hustons' place?"

"I'll do it before long." John's mind was on the Hustons too, but for a very different reason.

Richard began complaining that he didn't feel well enough to go to work. He stayed around the house a lot, but usually got dressed and left the house before the coal train began bringing the miners down from the mine.

This was a typical day — Richard getting dressed and leaving shortly after mid-afternoon. As the train slowed for John to jump off, Bill Huston yelled, "Hey, Shorty, I almost forgot; Dad said he could help you fetch the stove tomorrow bein' as how it's Saturday." Then he saw Pinky in the doorway, "We cain't have a pretty little thing like that gettin' cold now, can we?"

Richard stepped from a clump of scrubby oaks.

"What did you say to my wife?" There was an awkward pause.

"Slim! . . . you feelin' better? . . . I ain't seen ya' around . . . Uh, I didn't say nothin' . . . just passin' the time o'day."

Richard had reached the coal train and John leaped on him and wrestled a knife out of his hand. Without the knife, Richard whirled and slapped Bill across the face. It happened so fast, everybody was shocked and completely off guard. Bill Huston brought his grimy hand tenderly over his smarting jaw.

"I'll kill you for this," he said softly. Richard turned and disappeared as quickly as he had come. The driver swished the reins and the mule carried the cars on down the mountain with only the creaking wheels breaking the silence.

The mountains echoed the awareness that blasted down through the stillness: "OUTLAW TERRITORY." All the dinner

56

invitations and the friendly neighborliness did not dim this glaring fact!

John drew a long breath, "That settles it . . . start packing!!"

"Why? You got nothing to do with the trouble Richard got himself in." Lizzie put her hands on her hips as if preparing for a long argument.

"Start packing . . . I'll be back." John left in a trot!

Pinky had left running in the direction that Richard had gone. The sun was already behind the western slope and the thick wooded area began darkening. There was nobody for Lizzie to argue with. She went inside and started getting their few things together.

Pinky hurried in, wiping sweat from her face. "Miss Lizzie! Why did he do a fool thing like that . . . they'll kill him!! . . . What you doing? . . . Packing?"

Lizzie sighed heavily, "Yes, I guess so."

"Well, what if I can't find Richard. . . ? What am I gonna do? Can I go with you? I got a little money saved. . . . I'd be scared to death to try to stay here — no tellin' where Richard is . . . I just cain't stay here by myself, Miss Lizzie, can I please go with you?" Pinky kept looking out into the darkness as her anguished thoughts pushed through her tortured lips.

She waited for an answer from Lizzie, but Lizzie was taking her time trying to choose just the right words. In spite of her fear and the present agonizing situation, Pinky was still basically an immature child who could not be trusted to act in a responsible way at times. The situation here had not been the kind that allowed a lot of "shilly-shally, dilly-dally" carrying on, and part of the trouble had undoubtedly been Pinky's own fault. Pinky realized that Lizzie's hesitancy meant that she was not entirely welcome to come along.

"I never wanted to come here, anyway . . . no place to go . . . nothin' to do . . . scrouged up in this cracker box. I might'a been able to make out if I had stayed in Embodin . . . Where in the hell can Richard be?" and she ran out into the darkness calling his name.

Flossie Rainey and her little brother, Lee, were getting "last tag" from Sally as they brought her home from an afternoon

57

of playing. John caught up with the trio as they ran back and forth.

"You young'uns better scamper on back home now, it's gettin' late. Hurry up, Sally, wash your hands and eat."

"I already had supper. Mrs. Rainey had beans and ham and cornbread and. . . ."

"All right, but wash your hands anyway." John hurried into the little room where Lizzie was bustling about tying bundles.

"Where did you go? Did you see Richard? Did you hear anything?" Lizzie asked as she began pushing things aside to fix John's dinner. "It's cold; I'll see if the fire's gone out."

"Never mind, I'll eat it cold . . . we don't have time."

Seeing the food, John realized that he had not eaten since noon. Chewing large mouthfuls, he explained to Lizzie, "I went to get my pay and to make some arrangements with Mr. Collier. I didn't see Richard and I didn't hear anything much. . . ."

"What do ya' think will happen? Do you think they'll do anything? I mean, didn't nobody get killed or even hurt — seriously. . . ," Lizzie asked, and John stopped chewing. They looked at each other then, because they both realized that they were talking about terms whose definitions fluctuated with the circumstances.

"I understand," John went on, "that they usually will force each party to accept a gun, and then it's whoever draws first — I say *usually*, because nobody knows what will be done this time, and I'm not waiting around to find out." John finished his supper, pushed the stool back, and stood up. There stood Sally, wide-eyed and perplexed. "Get your daddy a drink of water." He had forgotten she was there. They would have to change the tone of the conversation. While Sally stepped out to get a dipper of water from the bucket on the shelf, John said quickly, "Only train out of Harlan goes to Cincinnati; we'll be on it!" He drank thirstily and handed the dipper to Sally.

A dejected, exhausted Pinky blocked the doorway. "Did you see Richard anywhere, Mr. Parker?"

"No, Miz Johnson, I didn't see him."

Pinky stumbled in, leaned against her bunk, and buried her face in the quilts as sobs shook her body.

"I don't know what I'm gonna do . . . ain't no way for me to stay here by myself . . . Sure wish you all would let me go with you; I got some money saved up."

Pinky looked so bewildered and frightened that Sally, still holding the dipper, went over and took her hand.

"It's not so much the money . . . I guess I could manage . . . it's . . . well, your husband is hot-headed and he's mad now and not thinking straight. I don't want him accusing me of taking you away."

"But I cain't stay here, Mr. Parker."

"I can understand that . . . 'course I must say, you didn't help matters. It never pays for a married woman to get too friendly with other men. . . ."

"There wasn't nothin' between me and Bill Huston . . . NOTHIN' . . . Richard got mad 'cause I would get asked to dances once in awhile 'cause everybody knows there ain't enough girls to go 'round."

"Miz Johnson, you don't have to explain a thing to me. But you see what it all led up to . . . never pays!"

Pinky began to cry again and John felt sorry for her, but he couldn't bring himself to ponder her problem further when he still had no plan for getting out of Nolansburg to Harlan.

Lizzie was trying to harness her thoughts. She wanted a sensible reason for doing what she was doing . . . packing their clothes, dresses she had made on Mrs. Rainey's sewing machine, the few ragged things that she had brought from home still good enough to save . . . two quilts, the box with her gold and cherry glasses . . . John said they were going to Cincinnati! Leaving tonight! . . . Why? Richard was in trouble. We're leaving because Richard . . . somehow, that didn't make sense . . . NO . . . we are leaving because she did not want to be left here in this place with no law, no church, no school, having to depend upon the basic attitude of these people for survival.

"Pinky, you can tell Richard that I asked you to come with us. It wouldn't make sense to leave you here to fend for yourself," and Lizzie reached over and patted Pinky's shoulder.

"Thank you, Miss Lizzie." It was as if Pinky had been

59

given a mild shot of electricity, she gathered her belongings so quickly.

Nothing was said after Bill Huston's statement to Richard. The coal train stopped to let Dave Rainey off at his place and the men waved half-heartedly. Dave washed part of the coal dust off and changed his clothes. Ignoring both his wife and his supper, he harnessed his favorite horse and headed out in a gallop. Rainey drew his reins in tight and dismounted almost before the bay halted. Ted Huston, Bill's father, waited for him on the porch. In these parts, a man jogged unless he had important news. Rainey's mount had not been jogging.

"You heard?"

"No, what?"

"Where's Bill?"

"I dunno."

"Mount up, let's find him!"

"Is he is trouble? What's up?"

"Let's ride, we can talk on the way. If there's contact with the gang on the west slope, it could get nasty."

The two men had ridden together often in the early days, settling arguments and helping to create the kind of atmosphere that allowed the pioneers to live in comparative harmony. Ted Huston and Dave Rainey swung into their saddles and headed their mounts into the scrub that fringed the base of the mountain. They followed a path almost overgrown from lack of travel. Railroads had brought civilization too close and the possibility of recognition was too great, so the real outlaws had remained to themselves, up on the west slope. But the old-timers knew they were there like a festering boil, spoiling for a chance to make trouble.

". . . as I say, a pretty face, a hot head, and a blow struck with on-lookers. . . ." Ted's face was solemn.

"I don't like it. It's a sorry no-account thing to get all stirred up over, but I know my boy. He'll make good his promise unless we stop him." They left the path and started up the steep, rocky, perilous mountain. Time did not permit them the safer ascent.

Yes, Ted Huston knew his boy. Bill was a hard-working, good-looking young buck who thought he had a way with women. He was also a coward. Ted hoped that this last characteristic was not obvious, but he wondered why Dave was equally concerned about the west slope gang getting involved in this fracas. He said nothing to his friend, but he fervently hoped that Henly had had the presence of mind to close the liquor store. Their horses picked their footing carefully now as the shade of the mountain raced up from the valley from where they had come.

Pinky was on her knees looking for anything she may have missed when John froze!

"Hush a minute!" he whispered, grabbing the holster that hung above his bunk. Four pairs of ears strained to hear. There was the distinct sound of a wagon and of horses' hooves. How many? Who? . . . Why?

"Shorty!" It was the train driver's voice. Was this a "set-up?"

"Shorty, I'm alone. Mr. Henly told me to give you folks a hand. He said put everything you can on this here wagon. I'm s'posed to git to the railroad when it's good dark, and put y'all in a caboose."

The driver, known only as Frank, picked up as many bundles as he could carry and started for the wagon. He had not said a word about haste, but watching him striding toward the wagon, the message was clear.

John's thoughts pieced the scheme together. Mr. Collier must have told Mr. Henly to make the arrangements. He felt good. Mr. Collier practically owned the railroad that hauled the coal from Nolansburg to Harlan. Then he felt stupid and foolish, standing there holding a gun on his friend. He brought his mind back to the business at hand, holstered the gun, and grabbed the rest of the boxes.

"Leave a light," Frank suggested. Lizzie put the globe back on the lantern and climbed into the wagon. John fastened the door.

It seemed that the wagon was extremely noisy, rattling and creaking down the narrow byway. Tension lessened slightly when the railroad yard could be seen dimly in the distance.

61

With everybody carrying as much as he could handle, only one trip from the wagon to the caboose was needed to get things settled. Frank reached for John's hand.

"Take care of yourself . . . I wish it could'a been different . . . I'll miss you folks." John, not being able to find the words to express himself, gave Frank's hand an extra hard grip and said "God bless you, Frank" as the two parted.

Sometime later that night, the little caboose shuddered from the impact of the freight as it made the connection, and the engineer was signaled, "We're ready to roll."

The passengers slept most of the way into Harlan. As the freight slowed down and began maneuvering to drop off the cars of coal destined for various points, the flagman indicated to John that there would be sufficient time to unload while the engine switched. They threaded their way carefully over the tracks, keeping a watchful eye for the engines. Some distance away they found the depot, and John checked the baggage to Cincinnati.

Lizzie, Pinky, and Sally found an obscure corner and waited, relieved that there were very few travelers in the depot. The bulletin board stated that the train for Cincinnati would depart in half an hour. John tried to walk casually as he went to the window to purchase their tickets.

"I want two tickets and one half fare to Cincinnati . . . no, make it three tickets. How much will that be?" John reached into his pocket and felt a hand on his arm. He whirled! There stood Richard! "I'll get Pinky's and mine," he said with a sheepish grin. As astounded as John was to see Richard, the thing that he felt most was relief.

"Richard! Where did you come from?"

"I came in on the same train you did. There's more ways to travel than one, you know."

The two men were glad to be together again. No one was taking into account the "rights" or "wrongs" of the affair at this point in time. The important thing was — Richard not being hunted down like an animal, or if he was, the chance of his being killed was decreased.

Pinky spied her husband half-way across the depot and she came running, crying and laughing all at once, "Richard!, Richard!" They embraced and swayed back and forth, silently conveying a message that their lips could not utter.

John went to find a place to get sandwiches and soda water, with Sally running after him.

Lizzie was struck with the thought, "My child . . . bare-footed on the streets of a big city like Cincinnati . . . I never thought much about it when grown people as well as kids went about as barefooted as rabbits all the time . . . but in a city—"

Sitting alone, Lizzie admitted that she was a little afraid. How could she find her way? She had never been in a city in her life except for the few hours spent in the depot in Bessemer.

"I fully intend to get myself a job. Sally is going to have nice things to wear like the other kids." She would have a chance to go to school. They would find a church and she and John would get to know people. . . .

Her meditation was interrupted by the announcement that the Cincinnati train was now loading. She looked at her own feet. These could hardly be called "shoes." On the other hand, John and Richard wore their work shoes and didn't look too much out of place, while Pinky had on a pair that had been stylish a few years ago but were still good. They joined the other passengers and boarded the train.

THE BIG CITY

The impersonal city of Cincinnati spread out before the bewildered travelers — John, friendly and talkative and unaware of the identity of deceit; Richard, shrewd and calculating; Lizzie, ashamed and constantly comparing the appearance of their clothing with that of others; Pinky and Sally, awed and excited.

Richard guided John in securing a place to live, a room with kitchen privileges. Having found a shelter for the Parkers, Richard and Pinky settled themselves in suitable quarters.

"Tell me again where to change and what to look for when it's time to get off." Lizzie was getting directions to her first job.

When Lizzie came up to be paid, the lady said, "Elizabeth, I like your work, especially your ironing. If you would like to come back next week, maybe you can get familiar with some of the things that work by electricity. Can you come back?"

"Yes, m'am, I would sure like that. I'm glad you liked the ironing."

Mrs. Duane Prinfort told her friends about the "new girl" and before long, Lizzie had three regular days on the Hill.

John found a job wheeling cement where a street was being repaired. They needed him for two days. He continued to look for work each day, but spent more and more time in the room on L Street.

Sally found a playmate who lived a few doors from the rooming house. Little Timothy was as lonely as Sally. Most children were in school, but they were older than Tim, anyway, and had no patience with him. His room full of expensive toys was too small for them, so when they bothered to come over at all they usually left behind a number of broken toys, along with a tearful Timothy. Sally and Timothy, however, got along beautifully, and they never tired of each other's company.

Lizzie was learning her way around the city. Today, as she left Mrs. Prinfort's house, she stopped off downtown. Sally had bruised her foot from walking on the pavement, and she had to have shoes.

"Ooooh, Mama, can I put 'em on? . . they're so shiny and pretty!" Sally took them out of the box and her face was as bright as the reflected light on the shoes.

"Can I put 'em on, Mama, please?"

"Yes, and then take the dishes down to the kitchen. Tell Mrs. Lewis I'll be down to wash them in a minute."

Sally began to wash her feet, struggle into her new socks, and push her feet into the slippers.

"They're so slippery, Mama, is that why they call them slippers?"

"No, I don't think so. Get the dishes and be careful, Hon."

Lizzie wanted a moment to talk to John alone. He was so depressed lately.

Sally gathered the plates, cups, saucers, knives, and forks. "Open the door for me, somebody."

Lizzie had already opened the door when she remembered that Sally had used the last water out of the big white pitcher to wash her feet. Wanting to re-fill it downstairs, she stopped to pick it up. Suddenly, she heard CRASH!!! She froze. John was suspended in mid air, not sitting nor standing, listening to the clatter of broken dishes and the clashing and colliding of knives, spoons, and forks as all of it tumbled down the long stairs. An ominous silence! . . . followed by a loud wail that triggered action. John and Lizzie raced for the door, reached it simultaneously, tried to go through unsuccessfully . . . backed away and tried again. This time John won and took the stairs two at a time until he reached Sally, lying at the bottom in the midst of the debris. She was fully conscious now, and all within a city block were aware of it. Fortunately, she was not seriously hurt, although her knees and elbows were skinned and she had other injuries, the most noticeable of which was her left ear torn partially away from her head.

"My slippers slipped, Mama, and I fell."

John carried her back up to the room while Lizzie rushed down to get a pitcher and wash basin full of water to cleanse the wounds and bandage them.

Sally healed, but John became more and more convinced that he couldn't make a living in this "hit and miss" fashion. He longed for the regular paydays he had had in Nolansburg. He counted the remaining money quite often, and today he realized it wasn't going to last much longer. While he was out looking for work, he had heard some interesting talk. He was thinking about it when Lizzie came in from her day's work.

"I hear they need some workers in West Virginia." The look Lizzie gave him was not encouraging.

"Doing what?"

"Digging coal." Lizzie knew that John was unhappy and that he had a right to be, but she was making some money now — an experience she had never had before.

"This is the third state we've been in since we left home. Seems like we ought to be thinking about settling down."

"Settling down to what? I haven't had a steady job since we got here and money's running low. . . ."

"The worst of the winter is over now and with spring coming. . . ."

John got up and stood looking at the grayish-brown brick wall stretching the length and breadth of the scene viewed from the only window in the room.

"Dog-gone-it!!" he said and shoved his hands deep in his pants pockets. Lizzie, knowing that he had just used his toughest swearing, changed the subject.

"Seen Richard lately?"

"I ran across him today. He's decided to stay here."

"Is he working?"

"I don't know. He says he's doing all right . . . hit a lucky streak. Pinky wants to stay."

"I had a feeling she would want to stay."

John went back to his point about work. The prospects of spring were not enough to dissolve his depression.

"I don't want to sound like I did in Bessemer, but I think I ought to go where there is work NOW, not wait to see IF things will open up here. I can dig coal better than I can work construction any day. Money is low."

Lizzie tried to offer a different reason for delay.

"There are schools and churches here. As soon as we get a few decent clothes, we. . . . Look, the two dollars a day I make up on the hill is the most money I ever made in my life. I can keep things going 'til you find something."

John was calmer now as he got down to basics.

"All right, you make two dollars a day. How many clothes can you buy after you pay the room rent every week? Remember, we have to eat. Ain't nobody sending you vegetables or meat like they did in Nolansburg. You pay for every bite that goes in your mouth here. We have had to take part of the money we

66

brought with us to make ends meet ever since we got off the train . . . when can we start to look for a better place to live?" and he waved in the general direction of the wall standing six feet beyond the window.

Lizzie was annoyed as she went to get Sally. Nothing had worked out the way she had pictured it. Cincinnati was hard to understand. You saw lots of people all of the time, but very few bothered to say "Good Morning." Sometimes those who spoke made you wonder what they really meant. She knocked on the door and Timothy ran to open it.

"You going to take your little girl home?"

"Yes, she has to eat her supper now. She's been over here all day."

"Let her stay and have supper at my house. Please!"

"Maybe sometime, if you ask your mama and she says it's all right."

The mother hurried to the door. "I would be more than happy to have her. Timothy is so crazy about her. She's the only one that plays with him without fighting him and breaking his toys. She's always welcome, anytime."

"Thank you. I'm glad they get along all right. Sally enjoys playing with so many toys."

"He's really starved for companionship . . . the toys . . . ," she waved as if to say they were of little consequence.

As Lizzie watched her, she felt that Timothy was not the only one "starved for companionship." The little boy was dressed as if he was expecting rich friends to arrive for a special party, and his mother's clothes were expensive-looking, too. Lizzie wondered what they did for a living as she walked back with Sally. With furniture like that in this part of town . . . Well, they couldn't live up on the Hill, she reckoned.

Her head tilted toward the Hill and her eyes sought the stars, so obscure in their misty distance. She felt a sudden need to build a wall of faith around the promise she had made to them as they had clustered overhead in an Alabama sky.

67

LIFE IN LITTLE LOGAN

For the first time, John and Lizzie had made their own decision about when to board a train. They had a little money, shoes on their feet, a fair-looking second-hand suitcase, and a little confidence.

They had seen mountains before — the gaunt, haggard mountains of Embodin whose rocky defiance drained a man's courage, and the Kentucky mountains, with veldtlush undergrowth hugging its sides so thickly that any awareness of progress was stifled like muted chords behind a wall of apathy and tradition. Now, as the train rounded curve after curve, it seemed to be saying, "You think those were beautiful? Just wait until I present the next scene!" Perhaps it was because they had traveled before mostly at night, in fear and desolation, that this journey was so breathtakingly different. West Virginia's mountains were a symphony in the springtime.

Out from the city of Logan, the Logan Eagle Mining Company had built a picture-book village of pastel houses for their employees. As the train began slowing down, they caught sight of the colorful cluster of houses, with a meandering stream that bent enquiringly near, following the railroad carelessly and then disappearing.

"STOWE, WEST VIRGINIA," . . . John read the name, making it sound almost like a song. He helped Sally and Lizzie off the train and started down the track to get the baggage. The baggageman had dropped everything off, the mail, and the packages, and waved to John as the train eased on down the road.

A man hurried out of the building that served as the general store, the post office, and the sheriff's headquarters. He extended his hand to John. "Welcome . . . I hope you plan to stay in our fair city." He laughed and spread his arms to take in the one visible structure.

"It may not be quite a city, but it's certainly very nice. How's chances for work?"

The man beamed. "Great! I thought you had come because

you saw our advertisement in the paper. We *need* miners. I'll call the super now, tell him you're here." He went into the building.

John turned to Lizzie, "I think we're going to like it here." "It is nice," she said, with a rare smile.

The man came to the door, "Come in out of the sun; they'll be here pretty soon to take you back to the settlement. Did you see it . . . a little way back?"

John assured him that it had definitely caught their eye, and the men continued talking. As Lizzie took Sally into the cool interior, her mind compared this general store with the Commissary in Embodin, Virginia. Pots and pans hung from the walls, bolts of cloth were stacked ceiling high on the shelves, and larger household items were seen in the rear of the store.

"There's a store a stone's cast from the settlement. It has food and some smaller items," the man explained as he and John came inside. He seemed anxious to have them like Stowe.

A pick-up truck came bouncing down the road toward the post office building. The driver turned out to be the superintendent himself, who jumped out of the truck, shook hands, and began to load the luggage on the truck and to help get Lizzie and Sally situated for the ride back to the settlement.

A closer and more leisurely inspection revealed colorful wild flowers and dogwood trees blooming in every crevice of the mountainside.

"There's an empty house right next to the bridge that you might like. By the way, my name is Tucker."

They were drawing up to the grocery store, a large, square-shaped building with the name "Gore and Son Grocery." They didn't take the time to go in. The truck couldn't be driven across the bridge, so the men started carrying things over to the little pink house trimmed in green. The bridge was about five feet wide and stretched over a shallow, rocky stream which Lizzie and Sally found ended in a half dozen steps descending to the level of the opposite bank.

The house had a little porch. The door led into a room with a heater. A door at the side of this room led into another room. And still another room was located at the rear of this one. All totaled, there were four rooms. The kitchen had two cupboards, a sink, and a stove. There were glass windows.

Lizzie kept walking around and around in the house. "A room for Sally, all by herself, a room to cook in. . . ." Lizzie had the happiest feeling she had had for a long time. She could not remember when she had been that happy. She sat down on the trunk and smiled, "Thank you, Lord."

The front yard was ankle deep in sand. She ran out to the back yard to survey the prospects of a garden. It was strewn with pebbles and sand, not much garden soil . . . but she could get some of the rich dirt from the nearby mountains.

Mr. Tucker was telling John that while they had the truck, perhaps they had better go back to Stowe and get the beds the Parkers needed to help them set up housekeeping.

Men were calling to each other as they came home from the mines.

Lizzie looked out. "I didn't realize it was so late," she said.

"We ought to stop and get something to eat," John said, joining Lizzie at the window.

"Let's have some ham and cabbage. Tomorrow, I'll make some biscuits and maybe bake a cake, since all I have to do is walk across that bridge."

John washed his hands and face at the sink, reached for his hat and walked out in the late afternoon sun. He saw Sally already very much at home, playing with the Browns' children.

John thought to himself, "This looks like the place to settle down." Whistling, he crossed the bridge to the store.

"I'll be with you in a minute. This is Mr. Parker, our new neighbor," Mr. Gore said to the several men in the store. They acted very friendly and many came to shake hands with John.

One man stood and looked at John with a quizzical expression. "You mind telling me if you were ever in the state of Alabama, Barbour County?"

"That's where I was born . . . near Clayton . . . Eufalla. . . ."

"Did you know a family by the name of Good?"

"I was raised up with Joe and Jack. I remember they had a sister. . . ."

"I'm Jack!"

70

Their amazement was overcome in lightening speed as they rushed to each other, laughing and pounding each other on the back. It seemed as though the questions had been rehearsed.

"What are you doing here in West Virginia? How long since you been home? How long you been here? Where is the rest of the family?"

They were now the center of a group who wanted to know all about the reunion. How long since they had seen each other? Where had they seen each other last? All this while, Mr. Gore stood with folded arms, smiling and enjoying every minute.

John was in high spirits as he flung open the door and invited Jack in to meet Lizzie and Sally. After some persuasion, Jack consented to stay for dinner ONLY if Lizzie would cook the corn and bacon he had bought and add it to the meal. Before the visit ended, Jack was promised the extra room and there was an understanding that he would become Lizzie's first boarder.

John was ready when Jack came by for him the next morning.

"Come on, if you comin' . . . Let's go, if you goin'," was Jack's symbol or trade mark. It was heard as regularly as the sun rose.

The advertisement put in the paper by the Logan Eagle Mining Company attracted a number of workers, some of whom were men with families, but most were unmarried and did not relish the idea of cooking for themselves. The few housewives were often asked to prepare special things for the bachelors. Any invitation to dinner was gratefully accepted by the single men.

Lizzie wrote to Ada and told her about the Logan Eagle Mining Company.

"You may find some of these single men willing to settle down. If you think you want to come, we'll send for you."

Ada's answer arrived in an envelope with a black border. "Henry died. We buried him last week. I wrote to you in Kentucky, but the letter came back. I'm really glad to hear from you and Brother John. I was so worried when I got the letter back. Is there any work for women where you are? I

71

don't want to be a burden on you all. I manage to make ends meet. I would like to come, but I can't sit down on you and Brother John. . . ."

No, there was no work for women here. Women could earn a little something by cooking cakes or pies for the bachelors. They didn't dress up often enough to need white shirts ironed. Ada would not come unless she felt she could look after herself.

Little Logan, as the settlement was called, was kept busy and happy, spinning tales to laugh at by night and working, either in the mines or in the homes, by day. Work went on almost around the clock, day shift and night shift in the mines.

Suddenly, frost warned that winter was cancelling the Sunday mountain hikes and the children's sand-castle building. The many fishing trips had netted nothing anyway. The black bass ignored every kind of bait or lure. They would look at it, swish an impudent tail, and disappear under a rock.

Jack Good and John spent many nights talking about boyhood pranks. John would rear back and let go with a "har-har-har," while Jack would squeeze out a tight little giggly sound while the tears rolled down his face.

Lizzie often wondered why Jack was not married and asked John about it.

"He doesn't seem to want to discuss it, and I don't insist."

Mr. Gore had an early shipment of toys and gifts for the Christmas holiday. The first snowfall resulted in such a volume of secret buying that a second shipment had to be ordered. Only four of the residents were young enough to be on Santa's list, but it took all the help Mr. Gore could give the old gent to keep his records straight. The bachelors were sending notes; the families were whispering and things were getting out of hand. Mr. Gore's father agreed to serve as a kind of a clearing house to avoid a great deal of duplication.

For the Parkers, it was the first Christmas they had looked forward to celebrating since the heart-rending episode in Alabama. Despite the help of Mr. Gore's father, Sally woke Christmas morning to greet three dolls, two toy stoves, and enough candy and fruit to last through February. It was the merriest Christmas the Parkers had ever had. Presents were exchanged and neighbors popped in and out of each other's houses. The Gores put up a Christmas tree with presents for everyone. Lizzie listened attentively as Mrs. Gore told Sally about the origin of having a tree for Christmas. It was necessary to have keen ears and sharp eyes if one wished to learn about unusual things. Lizzie found that it helped her to ease into strange customs and grasp new expressions.

The winter of 1917 was hard, cold, and brief. There was a record snowfall that year. The men joked about the temperature, dressed warmly, and went happily to the mines through it all. It was not unusual to hear of rabbits wearing hip boots or jay birds flying back home to get ear muffs!

THE FLOOD

Early March brought a warm wind to the corridor where Little Logan sat knee-deep in snow. The combined results of rain and the breath of early spring sent water cascading down from the mountains that circled three-quarters of the valley. When the rain continued into the fourth day, Mr. Gore began to worry. The store was built on the south side of the stream near the railroad as it skirted the mountain. The south bank was at least twelve feet higher than the northern bank. The stream was deeper and swifter on the south side. Mr. Gore reasoned that if the water eroded that twelve-foot bank, his store would topple. No one had suspected that the innocent-looking rocky water bed, measuring less than two feet deep at its northern bank, was capable of eroding anything. But Mr. Gore had lived in Little Logan longer than any of its present inhabitants, and he was worried. When he was asked why he had built the store flush with the bank, he answered, "It had at least twenty feet out back when it was built. A big chunk fell off and washed away about eight years ago."

The relentless rain saturated the stretch of sand that reached the base of the mountain. Water jounced and jiggled in every depression in the ceaseless downpour.

John and Jack were working the night shift, and Lizzie and Sally had gone to bed early. The rain had cut down outside activity, and more and more orders were being left for special things to eat. Tom Winston wanted a pot of navy beans cooked with salt pork, Hinton Jackson wanted a large peach pie, which he intended to eat all by himself, and Albert Shaw wanted chicken and dumplings. Lizzie needed time for buying and preparing all these things. She might have to borrow Jeanny Brown's big pot.

"MOVE OUT! . . . MOVE OUT!! . . . MOVE OUT TO HIGHER GROUND!!!" It was Mr. Gore's voice. "Mrs. Parker! Mrs. Parker!!"

Lizzie sat up in bed, trying to determine if she was dreaming. Then she heard the deep, tremendous roar, and Mr. Gore, wearing hip boots, splashed up on the porch and banged on the door, continuing to call urgently.

Lizzie sprang out of bed, and pushed the button to turn the light on. There was no light. Pulling a dress on over her nightgown, she raced to wake Sally, pushed the sleeping child's arms through sweater sleeves, and ran to open the door. She was met by the increased volume of the roar and the spray from a wave that had been rebuffed by the facing of the porch.

"Hurry! Put your valuable things in the trunk . . . I'll put it on the bed . . . get some warm things, a blanket or two . . . . . HURRY!" Mr. Gore was moving awkwardly about in the dark in his boots and heavy oil slicker. Sally rubbed her eyes as she stood leaning in the doorway of her room, watching her mother darting about. She saw Mr. Gore help her mother lift the trunk and place it on the bed. Mr. Gore then lifted Sally on his shoulders and started for the door as Lizzie snatched a quilt off her bed and tucked it around the child.

"We don't have much time, Mrs. Parker; that's as safe as we can make it. Lock your door!"

Outside was unreal. Where the yard had been, people were wading, waist-deep, calling out to make sure all members of

74

each family were accounted for. Someone held a lantern, shielding it from the wind-whipped water.

"HIGH GROUND," the lantern-holder hollered above the roar of the storm. People began following the flickering light to the mountainside.

Children were crying and clinging to the skirts of their mothers and mothers were patting the heads of their children without assurance. Lizzie was thinking that she should have put a few more things in the trunk and taken the time to get a little food, but she just took Sally's hand when Mr. Gore put her down upon reaching the side of the mountain. Water climbed stealthily up the stalks of the bushes that fringed the mountain as the wind bent the trees to its will. It also pushed the sound of Mr. Gore's voice back into his throat.

"Are we all here and accounted for? How many are working the night shift?" he asked anxiously, and began checking off names. Attention was diverted to a new sinister sound . . . a straining, creaking sound ending in a thunderous crash!

"My God!! The bridge is GONE!!!" Mr. Gore instinctively turned toward his store to investigate, only to be discouraged by water up to his armpits.

It took a few minutes for the impact of the situation to seep through the befuddled minds of the refugees . . . They were now cut off!! The bridge had been their link to the railroad, the post office . . . to the outside world . . . it was gone. They were alone, huddled on a mountain. No one knew how high they would have to go, or how long they would have to stay. The realization was mind-reeling!

"How is Papa going to know where we are, Mama?" Sally asked, looking up into the rain-soaked night.

Lizzie bent down and hugged her child. "He'll find us . . . he'll find us." But the unspoken thought in Lizzie's mind was, "How is the flood affecting the mines?" John had told her about the underground springs and the leaking overhead.

"First thing I noticed when I came here was all that sand . . . the little rocks so round and smooth . . . I knew this was all a part of a river bed", Sam Winston was talking. He had a kind of an accent like Geetch. Sam was from Louisiana. "Just a matter of time 'til the river claimed its own."

They moved from time to time to escape little streams rushing down to join the water at the foot of the mountain. There was little talk; each was busy with his own thoughts. Finally, the wind began dying down. There was less thrashing of the trees. The rain was not pounding as viciously now, and the edges of the humps of the eastern mountain were turning slightly gray.

"LOOK!!" . . . "Up there! It's the miners!!!" Near the crest, one could see tiny pinpoints of light weaving in an uneven line, gradually descending toward the tense group clinging to the mountainside. The miners must have heard the "whoop of joy," because the lights were moving faster down the mountain.

Families were joyously embracing each other. John kept saying, "Thank God, you're safe," as he held Lizzie and Sally in his arms. "We've come through a lot . . . nothing left now but the fire." Although he didn't know how or when they were going to get off this mountain, somehow he felt that with the three of them together, they could make it.

The dawn came. Murky clouds scurried away, not bothering to look back at the devastation they had wrought during the night.

Mr. Gore strained his eyes, trying to see if his store was left standing. Yes! The store was there, with water sweeping about two or three feet above its foundation.

A twisted remnant of the bridge clung, inundated, to the south bank. The upper portion of a house, several trees, and other debris were detained by it. Obviously the constant lashing of the waves would soon tear it free. So, as neighbors crowded down to the edge of the water, trying to estimate the extent of damage to their homes, a gust of wind slammed a wave against the pile-up, ripping it free with a terrible din. The rushing waters carried it swiftly out of sight.

It was as light now as it would get. The winds soared upwards, pushing the clouds along. Mr. Tucker and some high-ranking mine officials were half way down the mountain before they were seen.

"Are you all right down there? Anybody missing?" They were running down to the miners and their families. Introductions were made to everyone.

"We're mighty glad you men made it down safely. We checked to make sure that everybody's out of the mines." The mine officials and the men began serious talk about repairs and cleaning up. A bridge would have to be built and engineers would be sent out from Huntington as soon as the flood waters receded. Talk went on about how to get along in the meantime, and the assurance was given that all costs would be taken care of by the Logan Eagle Mining Company. After about an hour, the officials and Mr. Tucker left and continued on toward the post office at Stowe.

The houses nearest the mountain bore evidence of less damage than the other homes, and the occupants went to work with the help of neighbors to scrape out the mud, wash and scrub the floors, clean whatever could be used, and throw away all the rest.

Around a small bend and on an elevated mound was a nine-room boarding house that had not been used for years. The flood had barely reached its floors. Mr. Tucker spoke to John about opening the boarding house to accommodate the single men in the community. The company would furnish it and arrange to collect the board and room fee and turn it over weekly.

"What do you think about it, Lizzie?" John asked.

"The company handling the room and board rent sounds fine, if you can trust the company. I don't want any hassle with these men about money," Lizzie answered.

It had come to be known that she had a way of turning out tasty food, so with Lizzie in the kitchen, keeping the boarding house full was not going to be a problem.

"We won't know if it will work or not unless we try it. I'll tell Mr. Tucker that it will be all right," John said.

So instead of cleaning up the little pink house near the bridge site, John and Lizzie moved into the newly-furnished boarding house, along with six of the single men as boarders.

PICKING UP THE PIECES

Ada received another letter from her sister, Lizzie:
"You could help me with the cooking and washing and we could share the profit. Let me know so we can send your fare. It's getting warm now and the place is so pretty. We've almost forgot about the flood . . . Let me hear from you. . . ."

Ada's answer was vague. At least, it would have been vague to a less knowledgeable person than her sister. To Lizzie, it simply meant that Ada was currently interested in some young man who she hoped would propose, and that she would accept without hesitation . . . That was the unsettling part — Ada would accept without hesitation. Lizzie began to worry, but running the boarding house left her little time for it. Meals to prepare for two shifts of workers, linens for eight beds to be washed by hand weekly, plus keeping one or two men in line occasionally took most of her time.

The new bridge was sturdier but not strong or big enough for motor traffic. The stream was now contained in a narrow bed, flowing innocently near the south bank, leaving the stones, pebbles, and sand as dry as desert wasteland. However, the question near the surface of every mind was, "When will it happen again? Will the river claim its own next spring?"

Life in Little Logan had settled back to a day-to-day routine bordering on hum-drum when a young boy wandered into the settlement — a young giant, who thought his six foot height could conceal his lack of maturity. His smooth face with hopeful fuzz was one of the lesser things that established the fact that he was only a boy. The young man's feet were raw. It was assumed that he had walked a great distance. It was also evident that he did not lie convincingly. No one believed his

78

answers when he was asked his name, where he came from, or what the circumstances were that had brought him to Little Logan. He was anxious to work and seemed willing to go to any lengths to get the opportunity. Most people distrusted him and went out of their way to avoid him. Lizzie, however, felt she could not deny him a chance to prove himself.

"Oh, I don't know, I guess he reminds me of my brothers. Lord only knows what kind of tight places they've come through. Somebody gave them a chance." And Lizzie's mind would go back to a night on a train and a strong brown hand touching her shoulder, "Lady, lady, I paid it . . . you won't have to get off."

"Legs," that was the nickname they gave the boy, started working as soon as his feet were well enough. He was a good worker. There were indications of grudging acceptance on the part of many of the neighbors, and noting his gratification was like watching a Great Dane puppy.

This Saturday was Lizzie's pay day. The company's messenger brought the money covering a two-week period of room and board.

"I could have sworn that I left it on the kitchen table when I dashed out to catch Mr. Johnson to ask him to carry my letter to the post office for me. There wasn't a soul at home that I know of. I might have stayed a few minutes talking to Mrs. Johnson. . . . When I got back, it was gone! The bag and all!"

Later it was discovered that Legs hadn't come in for dinner either that evening or the next day, which was Sunday. Few expected him to show up for work on Monday, and he didn't. Lizzie was heartsick, both for losing her money and for losing confidence in the boy.

It was a close squeeze to feed her boarders for two weeks on the little money she had managed to set aside. On Wednesday of the second week, Lizzie was desperately trying to stretch meals. She was preparing a stew that had more potatoes than it should have and steeling herself for the comments she knew she would hear at the dinner table.

79

The front door creaked; she looked up into the sheepish eyes of Legs.

"Here, Miss Lizzie," he said, holding the money bag out to her. "I didn't spend it all . . . I don't know why I did it . . . but I had to come back. I couldn't treat you like that." He spoke haltingly. "Please forgive me; I intend to pay every cent back. I don't know why. . . ." The boy was crying and Lizzie's eyes were stinging.

"Where have you been?" then remembering his reputation for lying, "Never mind, I'm glad you came back. How do you know you can get your job back?"

"I figure if you write a note and ask them to let me work to pay you back, they would let me do it."

"And if they do, maybe you'll get your pay and just leave."

"No, mam! I want them to take out your money and give it to you like they do the room and board money."

Lizzie thought about it for a minute. It sounded reasonable. Of course, she would have to get John to write the note to Mr. Tucker because she had only learned to write her name well enough for others to read. She was so glad to have her confidence restored. Now she could give the neighbors the "I-told-you-so" look that they had been giving to her.

CAVE-IN AT THE MINE

Spring dissolved into summer and the predictions for heat waves were as outrageous as the predictions for the winter cold had been. The dozen sheets were rippling in a gentle breeze while Lizzie relaxed before starting dinner. Suddenly, she jumped to her feet and raced outside to get her sheets. She thought she had heard a distant roll of thunder. But Lizzie, along with several neighbors, looked up into a faultlessly blue sky. There it was again, an ominous rumbling. . . . "THE MINES!!! MY GOD, THE MINES!!!"

Lizzie's knees refused to carry her weight. Her feet turned to lead. She watched helplessly as neighbors passed her by with fear etched on their faces. She stumbled toward the mines, praying in a state of numb disbelief, compelled to keep going, yet holding back in dread. She came in sight of the mines. Dust that had been belched from the troubled drift mouth still hung suspended over the small knots of anxious people. Lizzie's eyes searched for John, blinking in the dust, and using the back of her hand to clear away the tears. "I'm dreaming, this is all a hideous nightmare . . . I'll wake up any minute now. . . ." But the fear was real, the finality of death . . . the unfulfilled hopes . . . the pain . . . the suffering clutched her heart and impaired her breathing. . . . It was REAL.

"Oh, NO! NO! NO!" A woman's heart was breaking as her screams tore through the dust-ladened air. John was one of the men who was bringing the body out. Lizzie put her arms around Mrs. Lynn and shared the thrust of the grim tragedy, in spite of her relief in knowing that John was safe. Each individual paid his tribute at the altar of close friendship. Thus began an unending slice of time that started with an ominous rumble and extended into eternity.

John was safe. Jack had perished, along with Mack Lynn and three others. Seven miners were injured, Legs among them. Some would never walk again. The days of making arrangements to ship bodies were extended nightmares. No one thought of Little Logan as a final resting place for the victims. And it took time to reach some of the families. Jack, for example, had never written any letters or received any mail. Contact was finally made with a cousin who came and took his body home. Legs' family put him in a hospital near where they lived.

John's spirit was crushed. "There's nothing more I can do here," he said as he looked out over the expanse of space where mountains met the sky. "I'll have to start scouting around."

The mines had been repaired and inspected. Notices had been posted to resume work. Lizzie planned her answer carefully. A night had not passed since the tragedy that did not find John, at some dark hour, sitting bolt upright in bed, drenched with sweat, and sometimes screaming. Lizzie wanted to cover her concern.

"This is not the only place . . . although it's nice . . . you got anything in mind?"

"No, it's got to be something else beside mining . . ." his voice trailed off. They were both thinking about the time in Cincinnati when he had stated, "I can dig coal better than I can do construction any day."

The next day, John suddenly called, "Lizzie!" She stopped making beds and came into the kitchen to see what it was he wanted.

"I think I'll take a little money and buy ten acres of land in Michigan."

"In Michigan?"

"Yes, Mason County." John had read an article in the paper, an ad by the Swigart Land Company. He was excited about it. Lizzie was happy to see his face light up and to hear the eagerness in his voice.

"They'll pay to have you come and look at the land . . . offer good for two weeks. Let's see, if I leave tomorrow, I can get within the two weeks deadline." John was comparing the paper dates with the calendar.

"I think I can make it . . . what do you think?"

"Well, you never know. 'Course you can't believe everything they say. They're trying to sell the land." Lizzie could have said more but she did not want to dampen John's mood. Getting away from Little Logan would be good for him, and she showed how she felt by going into the bedroom, getting the old suitcase, and dusting it off.

With her husband gone and two of her boarders in the hospital, Lizzie found time to re-evaluate Little Logan. It had no schools and Sally was getting older every day. It had no church. No minister had been around to say a word of comfort during the unforgetable tragedy. No doctors or dentists were nearer than Logan, and the nearest hospital was in Huntington. Lizzie's hope grew stronger that he would find something suitable in Mason County, Michigan.

A letter came from John. He wanted to come back through Detroit. He heard that there was plenty of work there.

"Doing what?", Lizzie wondered.

Memory is a peculiar thing. Getting a letter from John brought back all the fears, anxieties, and hopes she had experienced in York and Embodin. This time, the strongest emotion was hope, and Lizzie thought that was good.

With a handful of days left in July, Lizzie succeeded in closing the boarding house, packing, and leaving Little Logan to join John, who had been hired at the American Car and Foundry in Detroit.

SETTLING DOWN IN DETROIT

President Wilson went to Paris in 1918, and Lizzie went to Detroit . . . Detroit, struggling with traffic rattling noisily over brick paved streets, two years before the first traffic light was installed at the foot of Woodward Avenue.

It was not unlike Cincinnati, hustling, impatient, and impersonal. Everyone was tightly concerned with his own affairs. Lizzie and Sally sat and waited. John was not there and this vexed Lizzie and made her slightly apprehensive. She asked a man wearing a red cap about the baggage, but did not understand his answer. The time went slowly and a childish fear crept into a corner of Lizzie's mind. What if something had happened to John? What if she was stranded here in this strange city? How could she find out anything about John? Then she remembered the letter. She took it from her purse and read it again: . . . "I just went to see about work and they needed men so bad, they asked me to come to work the next day. So you get the Browns to help you pack up and you come on up here. I am staying with some very nice people. . . ." And there was the address: 1926 Russell.

John thought Lizzie's train would get to Detroit about five-thirty or six o'clock. He didn't want to lose a day. The boss had made a long speech about how much it cost the company when men didn't show up on the job. He went far enough to say that it was mostly Negroes that couldn't be depended upon, especially after payday. John meant to prove that he could be depended upon. He would make the day and then have time to meet the train that evening.

"Come here, Sally, let's go out and look around. I'm tired of sitting in here." Sally came skipping over to her mother, took her hand, and they went out into the late afternoon sun. Taxis careened and honked horns, horses clopped along pulling wagons and carts, street cars clanged, creating what seemed like mass confusion. Lizzie did not dare attempt to cross the brick paved street, but simply walked part way around the depot and came back.

In the midst of a blaring voice announcing that trains were departing to various points, and the mad rush of people, bags, and bundles, Lizzie spied John. He was peering anxiously through the crowd, holding his hat in his hand, crushing it tighter and tighter as his tension grew.

"There's your Daddy."

"Where, Mama? I don't see Papa."

John had spotted them and was weaving through the crowd to get to them. It was a happy meeting, and John was full of talk about Detroit as the taxi threaded its way to the Russell Street address. It was good that Lizzie had not tried to find it on her own. At 1926 Russell was a large four-family flat. The family with whom John lived had the upstairs rear flat.

Mrs. Thistledon was coolly gracious. She reminded John rather pointedly that she could not accommodate a family, and that the little girl would have to remain in their room.

"I have a number of keepsakes and the furniture is almost new. I don't want to risk anything happening to it," she explained. Perhaps it was the expression on Lizzie's face that prompted Mrs. Thistledon to add, "You won't have much trouble finding a place . . . we'll help you look out for one." She smiled as she showed Lizzie how to work the gas range and the dishes she would be permitted to use.

"I'm awful fussy about my kitchen," and Mrs. Thistledon looked at Sally again. "I'll have to insist that the floor be kept just the way it is now. So wipe it up after each meal. Then any grease spots can be cleaned up right away. I keep the brush, pail, and kneeling pad in this closet. A mop won't do."

John was embarrassed and puzzled. He had told Lizzie what wonderful people the Thistledons were, so out-going and friendly, and now before he could get his wife and kid in the house, Mrs. Thistledon turned a completely different side to them.

Lizzie scrubbed the kitchen floor three times a day. Sally stayed in the room and John lost no time looking for a place to live.

A few weeks later, John saw furniture being loaded on a coal wagon and asked where he could find the landlord. He was able to locate the man in charge of rentals and arranged to rent a flat at 2019 Russell, just down the street from 1926.

By now it was time for school opening, and there was much to be done. Many stores dotted Russell between Holbrook and Philadelphia. Most of them had large Jewish symbols splashed on the plate glass. These store owners were hard to understand and they had difficulty understanding Sally or Lizzie when they came in to buy something. By using much gesturing and pointing, sufficient second-hand household goods were bought to furnish the two bedrooms and the kitchen. Lizzie learned that the better homes had a "living room" which was used for sleeping only in case of emergency; for this purpose, duofolds were very much in demand.

It took time to learn the way downtown, and at the moment Lizzie didn't have much time, so Sally was outfitted at the stores on Russell Street. A new gingham dress, long white stockings, a ribbon for her hair, a slip with a little lace trimming, and some polish for her shoes.

"Do you have any records from the school she attended last?" They were at the Moore School. The clerk had some papers on a table. She was going to write down information about Sally, and she waited expectantly. Lizzie wasn't sure how to answer.

"Well, she . . . this is the first school she'll be going to."

"How old is she?"

"She was seven in June."

"And you don't know what grade she's in?"

"She can read and she can count up to a hundred and she can . . ." The clerk interrupted, "Mr. Edinborough?" she called to someone in a small room with walls of frosted glass. A tall, gray-haired man came out. The clerk said, "Here's another one. Name's Parker."

"Step in here, please, Mrs. Parker . . . bring the child with you."

Sally had been watching the other children. A loud gong sounded and suddenly the building was full of laughing, jolly, and very well-dressed children. The little girls wore dark skirts, white blouses with lacy frills, pink or yellow socks with black patent leather slippers . . . the kind Sally had had in Cincinnati when she fell down the stairs.

"There were no schools in . . . in . . . ?"

"Little Logan. No, sir, and none in Nolansburg, either."

"We'll have to try her out in a few rooms before we know where to place her." Mr. Edinborough was getting up and indicating that Lizzie should follow him. He stopped a little way down the hall.

"Miss Zimmerman, this is Mrs. Parker and her daughter, Sally. I'm not sure that she belongs in your room, but I'm placing her here for a few days. At that time, the determination will be made as to whether or not she will remain here. You can explain the routine schedule."

Mr. Edinborough turned to Lizzie. "She'll answer whatever questions you may have . . . I must get back to the office."

Sally noticed that her mother had offered her hand when Mr. Edinborough said, "This is Mrs. Parker . . ." Miss Zimmerman, however, had kept her arms tightly folded and pretended not to see the outstretched hand as she explained, "I don't know if Mr. Edinborough told you about the grade system. We promote children between grades — I mean, they don't go all the way from first to second, but we pass them from 1B to 1A — and then 2B to 2A, 3B and so on. This is a 1A class. We'll see if she can do the work." Sally disliked her.

Two days later, Sally was sent to the office with a note. Miss Zimmerman wanted Mr. Edinborough to know that Sally was too advanced for her class and suggested Miss Tremont's room as being the grade she would fit into best. Thus, Sally was taken from the 1A and put into a 2B room, where in fact, she did fit very well.

PROBLEMS WITH SCHOOL

"Come ye that love the Lord and let your joys be known . . ." Voices rose fervently following the chanted recitative. Russell Street Baptist Church was beginning Sunday morning worship. The deacons were carrying on the short prayer service before turning to the pastor for the sermon. The Parkers often attended the church since it was so near to them, located on the corner of Alger and Russell. They had not yet found a Methodist Church, and John and Lizzie had decided to join Russell Street Baptist under "watch care" until a church of their own denomination could be found.

It was through the association of music lovers like O. C. Williams, W. D. Lattimore, the Wardlaw brothers, Timothy and Columbus, Arthur Bell, and others, that the Morning Star Singing Convention was formed. This group consisted of people who appreciated and preferred shaped notes (Shaped notes differ from round notes or regular music in that each has its own distinct shape.) Choirs met every three months and sang *a cappella*. The songs they selected were sung by first singing the notes by name and then singing the verses of the song. These were memorable occasions that attracted throngs. John was proud that the Convention had held its first meeting in his home after the decision had been made to become an on-going organization dedicated to singing this kind of music. Lizzie sang soprano, John sang bass, while Sally was being taught the names and shapes of the notes.

Going to choir practice with her mama and papa was much more fun than going to school, even though there were no other children there. It wasn't the being in school that Sally minded; it was the running to avoid fights or beatings that she hated. Being somewhat a "loner," she had managed to evade membership in either of the opposing gangs. This was not easy on her. If Miss Tremont's class was quiet and orderly, they could be one of the first to be dismissed. When that happened, Sally could run across the street and wait inside the store until the gangs had clashed and had been broken up. Then she could very cautiously run the remaining three blocks home. Sometimes this strategy failed and Sally was beaten by one or the other of the gangs.

Early spring weather brought children swarming to the school playgrounds. At noon one day, Sally was waiting for the sound of the bell which signaled the time to enter the building. She was humming snatches of some of the songs which the choir was learning and keeping time by hopping first on one foot and then on the other. She was oblivious to the noises of the playground until she became aware of an unusual quiet. When Sally looked around, she saw the children smiling at her. When she smiled back shyly, they began laughing out loud. She didn't know why they were laughing, and her smile faded just as she felt the sharp pain of the first swift kick. She whirled. "Stop that," she screamed. "QUIT!!" Her shouts were lost in the raucous laughter that accompanied the thudding crunch she felt whichever way she turned. To be hit was one thing, but to be kicked was degrading. Sally was ashamed, humiliated, and angry as she tried unsuccessfully to defend herself. Someone caught her as she stumbled forward and saved her from a bruising fall.

"I wasn't bothering nobody," she kept repeating between sobs as she was lead into the building. By the time Sally had finished washing her face, the bell had rung and the halls were full of noisy children, some of whom had seen the kicking episode and were still laughing and talking about it.

"There was this big boy who pinned the 'Kick Me Very

Hard' note on her coat, so all the kids kicked her. I don't think the big boys should have kicked her, though. . . ."

Miss Tremont didn't insist upon Sally's participation in class work that afternoon, and said nothing when she saw that Sally's head was on her desk. It was still there after the class had left quietly. Miss Tremont touched the child's shoulder, "How do you feel?" Sally woke with a start and was shocked to see the empty seats. She thought she had done some awful thing.

"It's all right; I wanted to talk to you about what happened today. Today is April Fool's Day."

Sally looked puzzled.

"All kinds of practical jokes are played on people today. It's supposed to be fun. The children went much too far in what they did to you. But it was supposed to be a harmless prank. You may get your coat now."

The teacher was anxious to see if it was painful for the child to walk. Sally got out of her seat and, with only a slight limp, went to the cloak room and got her coat. Miss Tremont was relieved. She started to put her own coat on and lock the door when Sally began to cry again.

"What's the matter, Sally?"

"Mama's gonna be mad 'cause I got mud on my coat."

"You just tell her what happened. She'll realize that it wasn't your fault. Now hurry on home. Maybe you better let Mother take you to a doctor — just to make sure you're all right." Miss Tremont turned to unlock the door. "Perhaps I should write a note." She dismissed the thought. She didn't want to make a mountain out of a molehill. "I hope you feel better tomorrow."

Each step caused a throbbing pain at the base of her spine, so Sally didn't hurry. She thought about what Miss Tremont had said about April Fool's Day and remembered that not so long ago the class had had "Ballingtime." Everybody had brought little cards with red hearts saying "I Love You." "And I brought a candy bar," she recalled, as she relived the embarrassment.

The water in the tub had gotten cold. Sally stepped out and Lizzie inspected her child. She pressed hard, here and there, to find the tender spots. Sloan's Liniment was applied freely. Satisfied that no bones were broken, Lizzie would go to school tomorrow instead of going to a doctor's office.

"Come in, Mrs. Parker." Mr. Edinborough was looking at the slip of paper the secretary had handed him.

"Sit down, what can I do for you?" He was about to repeat the question when he noticed his visitor's lips were quivering as she struggled to speak. He pretended to scrutinize a very important letter that happened to be lying on his desk until he heard the stammering words forcing themselves through uncooperative lips. Lizzie stuttered. When she was angry, it was almost impossible for her to talk. She was agonizingly aware of this impediment, but today her anger overshadowed other emotions. The incident was told in jerking, halting phrases. The principal found himself straining to hear her faltering speech. As he listened, he realized that it had taken a great deal of courage for this woman to put herself through this anguish.

"I'm glad you came. It is important for the home and school to work together on problems like this. I assure you it will not happen again, or if it should, those responsible will regret it. Thank you for telling me about the situation." Then he added, "Please feel free to come in and talk with me again, Mrs. Parker."

A note was dispatched to all faculty members. That afternoon, an assembly was held in the auditorium. A very serious Mr. Edinborough informed the students that any child injured as a result of horse-play or so-called practical jokes would be required to report the matter to him. "And those who are responsible for the injury will be expelled."

As Miss Tremont's class marched from the auditorium, the principal beckoned to Sally to step from the line.

"Tell your mother that I am sorry about the trouble, but it will not happen again. You can always come to me or Miss Tremont if you have any more difficulty . . . I mean if anybody bothers you."

"Yes, sir," and Sally's smile was almost broader than her face. She still hurried home, but the tight "life or death" feeling was gone from the pit of her stomach. She felt that she had a friend who could do something about her tormentors.

ADA ARRIVES

Detroit was virtually bursting with people who had heard about the factory work and the good wages. World War I was in full swing. "TO HELL WITH THE KAISER!" signs were plastered everywhere. War materials were being manufactured day and night. Work was at a peak.

Thirty days rolled around very fast. John answered the knock on the door and mumbled a somber "Good evening." The caller had little time for causal conversation but counted the money John gave him and stuffed it into his pocket.

"It'll be ten dollars more next month, Mr. Parker."

"WHAT??" . . . "You went up five dollars last month."

"I'm losing money on you people. I could rent this place to four couples and make three times what you're paying. I can't afford to rent it any cheaper . . . ten dollars more next month."

John could either pay the extra money or vacate. But where could he find another house?

This practice forced many to sign contracts to purchase property, knowing that they would never own it. The arrangement protected the "buyer" from rent gouging. He could stay in the property as long as he kept up the agreed-upon monthly payment. Only property that needed "fixing up" was available for people like John who had so little money for a down payment. However, a house on Lumpkin was found with four rooms downstairs and four rooms upstairs. There was no bathroom on either floor. An outside toilet stood on the rear of the lot. John signed a contract to buy the property. Sally transferred from Moore to Davison School and Lizzie sent for Ada.

So much had happened since the sisters had last been together; it took hours of endless talking to tell it all.

"Aunt Vella wants to know about the prospects of boarders. She is thinking seriously of coming up here, too,"Ada said, looking around the house, and being impressed by the idea that Brother John was BUYING it. She still had those "puckish" eyes and her face could still light up in anticipation of childish delights — the same Ada, seeking the rainbow's end and full of hope. Lizzie was happy to have Ada under her wing again.

Very little persuasion was needed to bring Aunt Vella to Detroit. She came with her daughter's family. They stopped with Lizzie and John long enough to locate a house over near the Hudson Motor Car Company, on Connors Avenue, where a thriving boarding house arrangement was soon underway.

"CROWDED!" That was the word that described Detroit. Whole Jewish communities relocated so quickly that it seemed to occur overnight. Suddenly, the area around Dexter Boulevard was solidly Jewish; only the shabby neighborhood stores remained on Russell to remind one that Jewish people had ever lived there. Just as quickly, black families swallowed up the vacated houses. Because these families were younger and had more children, the Russell Street neighborhood soon experienced a population increase.

The Detroit schools adopted the "platoon system" to take care of the overflow. When a literature class was asked to sit two in a seat to provide space for Sally's fourth grade study period, she was introduced to the world of poetry, and fell in love with Longfellow, Stevenson, Sill, and others. Sally used this period not for study but to unfetter her imagination. Words like:

> "The twilight is sad and cloudy
> The wind blows loud and free
> And like the wings of sea birds
> Flash the whitecaps of the sea" . . .

created a scene and a mood for her. She had memorized the poem before many in the literature class, and her love for poetry resulted in her first stage appearance, reciting Long-fellow's "The Children's Hour" in the Spring Festival.

With Ada's arrival came substantial news that a brother, Thomas, was serving in the army and was possibly alive. The November signing of the Armistice had real meaning of a personal nature for the Parkers.

Lizzie had never said much about her family. Her father had died when she was about six, and two years later, her mother had followed him. Her brothers had scattered. Her sisters, except for Ada, had also died, leaving the two remaining girls to be reared by first one relative and then another, until they married.

Sizing up the men who came to call on Ada was a duty that Lizzie took seriously. However, any misgivings she may have had about Reverend Marshall Pearson were outweighed by the fact that he was a minister and needed a wife — a fact that he emphasized — and he seemed fond of Ada. A court-ship of seven months ended in a quiet marriage performed by Reverend Hall, a close friend of Marshall.

Shortly after they were married, Ada and Marshall moved to an under-developed area called "The Eight Mile Road." The rent situation had not eased, causing many families to undergo difficult and trying ordeals in order to have a roof over their heads.

"Got my notice today," John announced as he walked in, sweaty and tired. "Been expecting it ever since they stopped making all them tanks. No need for 'em, now that the war is over."

"War is over. You hear it every time you turn around, but not a soldier has come home yet," Lizzie said. She wondered if her brother was really alive or if she would ever see him again. They sat down to eat, after John washed up, to a rather silent meal.

With the factory job gone, he would have to hunt around for construction work. John was thinking. Would he be able to keep up the payments on the house? . . . How long? John, like many of the "home buyers," was faced with a dilemma. The house, badly in need of repair when purchased, became increasingly unfit for occupancy. If there was money available for repairs, should it be used for that purpose, when ownership of the property is not anticipated? There were two choices: They could continue to live in the house until the equity was absorbed and then move out and seek another deal. Or they could patch it up and hope.

While trying to reach a decision, Lizzie and Sally caught the flu. It swept through Detroit with epidemic speed. Ada came to help and was also stricken. John had to stay home to care for his family. The newspapers gave alarming accounts of the number of deaths resulting from the disease. There were reports that some of the bodies had had to wait for weeks for burial. The Board of Health warned against visiting hospitals. Doctors were working around the clock; many of them also became ill; and some died.

Dr. Clarence Melvin Clark had an office on Joseph Campau. He had known the Parkers and had looked after them when he had practiced in his home on Alger. Now he walked in, red-eyed and weary, and methodically examined each of his patients. Then he sat down and began writing prescriptions.

"I'm going to suggest that you write down the times their medicine is due and pin it on your shirt. Put each patient's medicine right by her bed. I'll be back tomorrow; call if there's a change. I'll get back as soon as I can." He was fumbling with his coat collar and heading for the door. John followed with his wallet in his hand.

"Thank you, Doctor. How much do I owe you?"

"No, you keep it. The medicine is going to cost a lot. You can pay me later. Be sure you give them everything they are supposed to have." It was late, but he consulted a list of names, put a line through "Parker," and left to continue his rounds.

John went about his duties as nurse:

Lizzie

> Brown liquid every two hours
> Red liquid every four hours
> Pink tablets every three hours
> Yellow tablets every six hours

94

Ada

> Red liquid every three hours
> White pills every three hours
> Brown tablets every four hours

Sally

> GARGLE EVERY TWO HOURS
> White pills every four hours
> Cough syrup when needed.

He would never have remembered all this while preparing soup, tea, and toast, and washing and changing beds.

When his patients were able to sit up and creep around the house, John realized that he was exhausted. Marshall came and took Ada home as soon as she was able to be moved.

Finally, the flu subsided. Statistics were quoted and people compared experiences. John joked about how he had managed his own private hospital, but he acknowledged to himself that he was afraid that of the three, Lizzie had been the most serious. She was a woman not easily pleased and given to fault-finding. He also conceded that she drove him to try a little harder, and furthermore, that he loved her.

EVICTED

A neat sign read "ALLEN'S TEMPLE A.M.E. CHURCH" in front of a store which was painted white. It noted that Reverend Brinson was acting pastor and gave the times when services were held. John and Lizzie found the little church on Cardoni and moved their membership from Russell Street Baptist. They soon became aware of a much less demonstrative atmosphere. This congregation had a robed choir, a pianist (called an organist), and a detailed precision in their service, which was predominately cool.

Reverend Brinson invited Reverend Pearson to preach one Sunday. His delivery was less intellectual and more emotional. He stood and looked out over the upturned faces:

"See on the mountain top
The standard of your God.
In Jesus' name I lift it up
All stained with hallowed blood"

The congregation's voice filled the church. After singing two stanzas of the hymn, he gave a sermon that was dotted with "Amens" in spite of heads turning and brows lifting.

Factories had quietly switched from war plants, tanks, and machine guns to domestic products and luxurious items. The buying public's appetite had been whetted and there was a huge demand for automobiles. Horse-drawn wagons and carts were being replaced by light and heavy trucks. Electrical appliances were appealing to housewives .Yet many workers were walking the streets both during and after the changeover. The idea that workers have a right to job security regardless of the whims of supply and demand gave rise to the push for unionism.

A violent period followed in which men were beaten and horses were spurred to trample crowds of protesting men. Some were thrown in jail while the subject of whether or not a company could be forced to allow employees to join a union was hotly debated.

John read the papers avidly. "A man would be a fool to get mixed up in a hassle like this," and he would show the pictures to Lizzie and Sally. One article said that it was rumored that Henry Ford would never allow any authority in his plant except his own. But the unions prevailed.

Meantime, oddly enough, there were sufficient people to handle the new equipment and machines. A tight apprenticeship program provided a select group for employment in the trades and in the factories. Without this training, a man could be hired only as one of the janitors.

Agreements between management and unions usually resulted in a delayed reactions and those affected gave voice to their disapproval as implementation of these agreements began. Many uneducated workers were told to take tests to determine their fitness for jobs. Even if passed, they still had to persuade the unions to allow them to join. The result of this arrangement was to create the "ins" and the "outs", the "outs" being those who were untrained, uneducated, and therefore unemployed.

Lizzie took the letters out of the mail box. She was too tired to try to read the postmark. She always had to wait for John to read the mail anyway. At best, she could make out "York, Ala." if it was stamped on the envelope, but little else. Maybe she should take the letter and let Mrs. Promantone read it. Lizzie recalled the second week she had gone to do the cleaning for the wealthy family.

"Elizabeth, do you mind telling me where you came from?"

"We came from West Virginia when we came here."

"I KNEW IT, I knew it!! I told my husband that you were not from the South. Anybody could tell that by the way you talk."

"But . . . I AM from the South. I was born in Alabama."

"I don't believe it . . . you're joking. . . ."

"No, we are from Alabama . . . York, really, out on the farm a few miles from York."

"Has anybody ever told you that you don't sound like the average Southerner?"

"Well, yes, I have had people say that to me."

"How far did you go in school?"

"I didn't get much schooling. I can read a little, but I can't write very well. I make out pretty good at figuring in my head."

"Are you sure you were born in Alabama? Oh, that's a silly question, but I just can't believe it. We had a bet on, and . . . well, I lose."

John came in from work. He was helping build the office building for the Braun Lumber Company on Davison.

"There's the mail on the table. Dinner will be ready by the time you get washed up."

"Where is Sally?"

"Next door, playing. She don't even know I'm home. I'm gonna give her a beatin' when she does come home. Breakfast dishes right where they was left this morning. She's got to learn that the kids next door and across the street have mothers who don't have to go out and do day work. They can play as long as they want to, but she can't."

John went into the bedroom with a pan of water to wash the cement and dirt off as best he could. He hoped that Lizzie would wait until he was away to whip Sally. It bothered him to witness the kid being punished.

Lizzie moved slowly today. She was tired. John took the few minutes before dinner to read the letters. Lizzie was bringing the food to the table now. Sally came running in.

"Mama, it's still so light outside . . . I didn't know it was this late . . . I . . . ."

Lizzie put the platter of potatoes and chops on the table and kimboed (hands on hips). "How many . . . also . . . times . . . have I . . . also . . . told you also . . . about leaving the b-b-b-breakfast d-d-dishes?"

"DOG-GONE-IT!" John exclaimed as he threw a business-like letter on the table. Lizzie's and Sally's eyes turned to him in amazement. He got up and walked over to the door and looked out. Lizzie motioned to Sally to pick the letter up and read it:

"Dear Mr. Parker:

Our records show that the payments on property located at 13146 Lumpkin·are in arrears. You are hereby notified that you can either pay the full amount of the balance of the purchase price agreed upon or vacate the property at the expiration of ninety days after receipt of this letter."

The meal was eaten in silence. John and Lizzie's thoughts were on the letter. What would be the next move? Sally wondered about it a little, but mostly, she was glad that Lizzie had forgotten about the whipping.

THE MOVE TO DETROYAL GARDENS

. . . . of Feathery Fern and Concrete Walls
They planted dreams between young oak
And waving feathery fern.
They waited in nearby huts
To watch the seasons turn.
Dream buds hung heavily
Until an early fall,
Then opened to gaze wonderingly
At a distant concrete wall.

"No matter how long you rent, you'll never own it. A car-load of rent receipts will not equal one deed and abstract." It was a convincing argument. Mr. Meadows would smile and look through his square-framed glasses, his eyes piercing your thoughts. "Land is not that hard to come by and nothing can give you the kind of satisfaction you get from owning your home."

Meadows was a salesman for land in a subdivision called "The Detroyal Gardens." Ada and Marshall lived in this sub-division and had urged Meadows to call on the Parkers. Since Marshall had no church to pastor, he was often away from home running revivals. Ada was lonely and extremely anxious to have Sister and Brother John as neighbors.

So it came to pass that John signed up to buy lot number 179, which was right next to lot number 178, owned by Marshall and Ada. The Parkers were tired of scrimping and sacrificing to pay on a leaking hull where the slop jars sent their pungent odors to greet them on the days when Sally forgot to empty them before going to school. It was time to make a move.

The interurban car whizzed along at about sixty miles per hour. It was dark orange in color and looked like a cross between a railroad passenger car and a city streetcar, powered by electricity, its pole sending out flashes of lightening siz-zling along the wire. The interurban cars provided service be-yond the city limits. The Parkers boarded a car at Log Cabin, where the city of Detroit ended, and the car stopped again at Eight Mile, where the Parkers got off. Then they began the three-mile trek on the sandy, shadeless road, devoid of any type of structure.

The Parkers walked into the Lockport School well after the service had started. Ada, not able to restrain herself, tiptoed over and hugged her sister and her Brother John and Sally. The little mission was pastored by Ada's husband, Marshall. The Lockport School served both Mt. Beulah Baptist Church and the Methodist mission, holding services on alternate Sundays.

When service was over, Ada introduced Mrs. Cornelia Davis and her two daughters, Mary and Nellie. Mrs. Davis had founded the mission. The Parkers were urged to join and help pull the little group along.

Ada was anxious to show off her garden and chickens. So even though the Parkers were still weary, they walked the half mile to the little house which Marshall had built.

"It's not much, but it's ours, and it sure beats paying rent every month." Marshall was right on both counts.

Lizzie's mind was busy as she allowed Ada to show her around. "There's an old saying," she thought. "If you start in the big end of the horn, you come out at the little end." Somehow she was going to have to pull her dreams from the sky and plant them on the ground. She sincerely hoped it would be fertile ground. Lizzie looked at the wild ferns waving gently on the next lot. There were no large trees to be cut down, just a tangle of undergrowth and clumps of bushes. It would do for dream planting.

Mr. Gaffney and Mr. Pickens were trying to start the old pickup truck. It sputtered resentfully at being disturbed, finally coughed, and rattled to a rhythmical protest.

"I guess, by Gannies, she'll make it," Mr. Gaffney announced. The Parkers piled in and waved "Goodbye" to Ada and Marshall.

This was peaceful country, with paths winding from neighbor to neighbor. Now and then, there was a trail that would eventually become a paved street. Lizzie and John, afraid to hope, shyly speculated.

The Braun Lumber Company's building was nearing completion. It was a sprawling, one-story structure. John dreaded the time when he would be told that they no longer needed him.

100

"There's not much left to do around here, except a few odd jobs," the boss said. John knew what was next and quickly suggested, "Maybe I can handle some of the odd jobs — I'd like to try."

"Gets awful hot, but most all the work is on the roof — few places have to be done over. We've had a lot of high winds." John was shown the places that needed repair and told the kind of material to use.

He was eager to show his gratitude for the extension of his stay on the job. He got busy, not noticing that the foot braces had been removed. Just before noon, as he reached for a tool, he lost his balance and slid off the building. When he opened his eyes, he became aware of a terrific headache and what he thought was a crowd of faces looking down on him. He was told later, however, that only three men had been trying to revive him. John remembered being asked, "How do you feel? Can you see? Do you feel dizzy?"

Lizzie was home that day. When she saw a man assisting John out of a car, she ran out to help.

"What happened? What's the matter? How did he get hurt? How bad it is? Did you get a doctor? What did he say?" They were assisting John into a chair. His eyes were closed because the light seemed to intensify the pain in his head.

"He was working on the roof and fell off," the man said. "He hasn't been able to tell us how it happened, but I think he'll be all right. It's just a short distance from the top of the building to the ground, you know." The man was leaving.

"I sure hope he'll be all right," he said again, "I don't think you need to worry."

About two o'clock, a man knocked on the door. "I'm from the Braun Lumber Company. May I see Mr. Parker?"

"He's sleeping . . . I don't know," Lizzie said.

"Maybe it's best that he don't sleep too much."

"I'll wake him up." Lizzie shook John lightly. He groaned. "A man from the lumber company wants to see you . . . Are you awake?"

"All right."

The man went into the bedroom and stayed a few minutes. When he came out, Lizzie asked, "Are you the company doctor?"

"No, but I think he is going to be all right."

"When are they going to send the doctor?"

"You will have to get your own doctor. You may not need one."

"Is the company going to pay the doctor bill?"

"No. Your husband just signed a statement releasing the company from any and all responsibility for his injury."

Lizzie was stunned. ". . . Do you . . . also mean to stand there . . . also and say that . . . also . . . you had my husband to . . . also sign his name to some paper . . . when he can't even . . . also open his eyes, hardly?"

"He signed it, Ma'am. And it WILL stand up in court, in case you all think about legal action."

Lizzie advanced. The man retreated to the door and left.

The Parkers lived out their equity on Lumpkin and moved to Fleming near Caniff for a short period. Swarthy, dark-haired men who spoke in a staccatto language frequenly had street brawls. One Saturday afternoon, one of them tore out of a house. A group charged down the street after the fleeing man. He dashed into a store and slammed the door just as one of the pursuers threw an axe that struck fire when it crashed into it. It was dangerous to be on the street. A free-for-all could develop without warning.

John was hired to drive a wagon delivering coal. The company was already in the process of changing over to trucks, trucks that would hoist the body and dump or funnel the coal through a chute into the basement, eliminating the back-breaking job of shoveling and wheeling. John didn't know how to drive.

"One more week and I'm through," he said in a tired voice. It was a quarter to ten. Lizzie started to warm up his supper. John looked around the room, and seeing nowhere to rest in his coal-dust covered clothes, he kept on to the bathroom to wash.

It hadn't been much of a job — working overtime without pay. If a delivery took you to Delray or to Grosse Pointe, you worked as long as it took. If you got stuck, you got out on your own time. And there were many, many unpaved streets in Detroit in the early 1920s. But taking all this into account, there was still a sense of loss at the realization soon he wouldn't have even that.

"We could take the rent money and order some lumber with it," Lizzie said. John's head jerked and he peered at her through soap smarting eyes, but he said nothing.

After putting things away in the kitchen, Lizzie came into the dining room and found John nodding over the evening paper. He had never been accused of fooling around on any job. He believed in giving a day's work for a day's pay. Looking at him, Lizzie's heart went out to him. He tried so hard. Too trusting and always ready to make excuses for the other fellow's shortcomings . . . That was the way John was and she guessed he would never change.

Suddenly a shot rang out, followed by the sound of running. Moments later, police were hammering on the door. John was dazed as police swarmed in, asking questions. "No, we just heard a shot and someone running . . . We have no idea who it was or what it's all about." They found the man they were looking for hiding under a porch a few doors away.

"He thought his wife was interested in a man who he thought had gone into the flat upstairs over the Parkers!"

That was enough.

Ada and Marshall cleared a room and the Parkers moved to the Detroyal Gardens at the Eight Mile Road.

A BITTER WINTER

Being scrunched up in one room would have to be tolerated for a very short time, just time enough for John to build a temporary house on the back of the lot next door. But there were immediate problems that had to be faced. First, the transportation — Lizzie had to get to work, and John, too, when he was able to find a job. And there was the question of school.

Lockport School was run by the county and was a lot like the rural schools in Alabama. One room, housing as many as six different grades, taught by one instructor. Lizzie was sure Mrs. Pearl Wright was a good teacher, but knowing the handicap Sally had had in starting her education, Lizzie wanted more assurance.

A visit to Aunt Vella and Cousin Ludie meant riding for hours on the streetcar and transferring twice. Aunt Vella moved a little slower now, but there was no other noticeable difference. She bustled about, still welcoming an emergency of any dimension.

"Now, Lizzie, you know that child is welcome to stay here."

"I wasn't sure you had any space."

"Oh, we're full, but nobody is using the duofold . . . if there's company, she can sleep with the grandchildren . . . no trouble."

Lizzie insisted upon paying Sally's room and board. It was understood that Sally would come home every Friday after school and stay over Sunday.

"I want a word with you," Aunt Vella said to her boarders. "My niece is gonna be staying here. She's a big girl for her age, but she's nothin' but a kid. Don't get any ideas, cause if you step out of line, I'll knock your block off. I don't want to have to remind anybody." They took her at her word.

This arrangement put Sally in the Carsten school district, which was predominantly white, and put the Parkers in a predominantly bad light in the Eight Mile Road community.

"They think their kid is too good to go to our school."

"Some folks don't feel right unless they're stuck up under white people." Nothing was further from Lizzie's mind, but she did not feel inclined to explain her position.

"They wouldn't understand anyway," she reasoned.

A dream is a luxury. It stands complete. It's void of pain, suffering, and the anxieties that come with the lapses of time between sections of fulfillment. The house was being built painfully slowly at the rate of fifteen or twenty dollars worth of lumber each payday.

Close observation revealed a subtle reluctance on the part of John to build this THIRD home. He was a man who showed a jolly surface, but within him were deep undercurrents. When he had signed the contract to buy the lot, he had envisioned a home somewhat like Lizzie's dream home, one built by professional carpenters. He saw himself coming home and relishing the sight of brightly-lit windows, opening the door to a beautifully furnished interior with several rooms, rooms in which to entertain his friends, who would come often to sing and enjoy refreshments.

As a boy, he had lived in a make-shift shelter. As a young man, his early marriage had been spent in a hut. He had endured Embodin and Nolansburg. He was now almost at the "Dog-Gone-It" stage, realizing that make-shift housing for him was far from being over.

Lizzie was irritable. It was bad enough facing winter having to depend on the independent bus owners getting her to Woodward Avenue so she could go to work. The additional thought of coming home to this one room, even in her sister's house, caused her to wonder. Many a morning, as she waited for a bus in the pre-dawn icy weather, Lizzie would ask, "Lord, how long will I have to wait? . . . Is this all I can hope for?"

Snow piled up on the roof of the little four-room house and accumulated during the severe winter. The roof sprang a leak over the bedroom occupied by the Parkers. One morning, Lizzie woke to find her quilts frozen stiff. Shortly afterwards, she suffered a serious attack of pleurisy.

Lizzie never tired of telling about what had happened during this illness. "I was supposed to go to Mrs. Staples that

Thursday. I woke up with a pain that took my breath. I tried to get up but I couldn't make it. John told me to get back in bed. He ran over to the farmhouse and called Mrs. Staples and told her I was sick. When I knew anything, Mrs. Staples and her sister was driving up out there! She brought me home once, but how she remembered the way, I'll never know."

The farmhouse had the only phone in the neighborhood. The family was white and lived about six blocks from Lockport.

"Well," continued Lizzie, "they started bringing stuff in — food, blankets, fruit — and then rolled up their sleeves and fixed me a meal! I knew they were nice, but I never dreamed they would do that sort of thing.

" 'We better go now, Elizabeth. We slipped off. Ed doesn't know we drove that old car. It's got no license, you know. We're going to put it back exactly like it was — he'll never know we came.'

" 'What if you get stopped by the police?' I asked.

" 'We'll tell them it's an emergency, and it is!' "

Ada, however, was not fond of retelling her experiences with some of the families she had worked for. During the time that Marshall was away running revivals, Ada looked for work. She didn't mind staying on the place. It was better than being alone, and not as hard as day work .

To get "references" was the hope of every worker, but with a city full of new, eager people, housewives made demands, and although some of them were extreme, they were sure that their demands would be met.

"Ada, when you finish the breakfast dishes, go down in the basement and unplug the sewer. You must have let something go down the drain — it's backing up down there."

"I don't know how to unplug no sewer — I'm sure I didn't let nothing go down the drain. . . ."

"Simply take the little cap off that's in the middle of the basement floor; run your hand down the opening and clean out whatever is making it back up!"

When Ada refused, she was told how lazy she was.

"That's the trouble with you people. You're afraid of a little work."

The real culprit turned out to be the roots of a tree that had grown into the sewer pipe.

Another lady had demanded that Ada wash the family car. The last place where Ada was employed did not have an extra bedroom, but they insisted that she stay on the place to be with an elderly member of the family. Ada slept on a cot in the unfinished attic. The temperature dropped to below zero one night, and Ada left with a cold that she still had. It caused her to cough a lot.

Dr. Clark pulled Lizzie through and she was hale and hearty by spring. He was not as successful with Ada. She kept on coughing.

Spring was surely on its way. The ground, which had been covered with layers of ice, was becoming visible in places where the sun could reach it. In a short while, the whole countryside would turn a yellowish, feathery green.

Jesse Snyder and Lizzie laughed until tears ran down their faces, telling about the time they had crawled on their all fours from Wyoming Ave. It was one of those foggy mornings when the moisture made the icy ground too slick for anybody to be able to stand up.

"I'd just about made up my mind that the bus wasn't gonna make it — and I didn't care, 'cause I wasn't for no pullin' and pushin' to get it out of the ditch that morning," Snyder was saying. "I looked up and there was Miz Parker. I said 'Good Morning,' but she hadn't seen me. It was so foggy, she turned around and fell. I rushed over to help her get up and I fell. Well, I tell ya, we would get to our knees and fall again. We fell so many times that it got to be funny. So we decided to try to get back home. After falling a few more times, we just stayed down and crawled on back home."

Although the weather was turning warm, work on the Parkers' house was at a standstill. Tension was easily built up in the four rooms that housed the two families.

Sally had been given a puppy. She named her "Frisco," a darling little black and white mixed breed with curly hair around her ears and big brown eyes that would melt stone. A kitten took up residence at the Pearsons' and Ada called him

107

"Casper." The puppy and the kitten became good friends as they grew up. During the summer, sometimes the quiet evening would be disrupted with Frisco's frantic barking. Casper would let out a "yowl" and the chase would be on . . . under chairs, across beds, under tables, up the curtains, across laps, leaving papers flying and torn asunder . . . back again until they were completely exhausted. They would then lie down under the kitchen stove, Casper resting his head on Frisco's middle, and go to sleep.

When spirits were low, or if there had been an argument, you could count on a show. Marshall would sputter and John would mumble about animals being kept under control or put outdoors, but they found themselves grinning in spite of the pretense.

One night, Casper was not around to eat his dinner. He had not shown up when it became dark and Ada was alarmed. She went out to find him. A faint "meow" could be heard. Ada listened. Casper was huddled on a limb near the very top of a large oak tree, meowing as if his last friend had died and he had been appointed to dig the grave.

Ada ran to get the neighbors after Marshall told her, "That cat's got sense enough to come down when he gets ready. I'm not going out there and make a spectacle of myself!"

"By Gannies," puffed Mr. Gaffney, "What's going on?"

Jesse Snyder, who lived right in front of the Pearsons' house, was the first to arrive.

"Son of a gun! They always pick the highest limb they can find." He was a two-hundred-pounder, and there was no thought of him climbing the tree. Mr. Donahoo came dragging a ladder which was far too short. By the time Mr. Pickens got there, Gaffney not only knew what was going on, but had offered to climb the tree himself. He was slender enough, but he was also 80. They decided against his offer.

There was a loud discussion about what cats did in situations like this. Everybody remembered a cat in a similar predicament, but all the cats did different things. Meantime, Casper meowed pathetically, Frisco barked and whined, and Ada wrung her hands.

The men went into a caucus: someone would stand on the top rung of the ladder with a long pole and try to induce Casper to walk down on the pole; failing that, they would try to push him off his perch. They didn't tell Ada about the "pushing" idea.

After many choruses of "Here, kitty-kitty — here, kitty!" Casper came hurtling down and hit the ground with a resounding THUMP! Ada rushed to pick him up, but he scampered away. She was heartened by his agility. A few minutes later, he limped into the house. Ada grabbed a box of salve and plastered Casper's fur with it to help heal his wounds. Casper, however, did not approve of this kind of medication and tried to lick it off. The taste caused him to growl and foam at the mouth as if he were going mad. Ada rushed to prepare warm water to bathe him; with this he was in complete disagreement. He was bathed in spite of his protests, however, and while Sally held an annoyed Casper, Ada cut out and made a pair of pajamas for him that fit snugly around his neck with a drawstring. The "Frisco and Casper Shows" were cancelled for a while.

SALLY STARTS HIGH SCHOOL

The Parkers moved into their house with only the first rough floor laid. "You'll have time during the summer to lay the second floor and varnish it," Lizzie told John. Looking through the wide cracks to the ground under the house reminded them of the little house in Alabama — how many miles away? . . how many years and hopes ago?

John still hummed or sang "On Jordan's stormy banks I stand." Now Lizzie found herself singing, "I'm going to trust in the Lord 'til I die."

By 1924, forty-seven families had moved to the Eight Mile community. 1924 . . . a year to give a helping hand to miracles and dreams that were overdue. Residents were growing tired of kerosene lamps, outdoor toilets, and pumps.

Lizzie had invited company for Sunday dinner. On Saturday night, the temperature dropped and the pump froze. None of the Parkers went to church that Sunday. John built a roaring fire in the kitchen stove. Sally raked up buckets of snow to be melted. Lizzie was running back and forth to Ada's house to get clean water to use for cooking while the thawing operation continued in the small kitchen. Everybody had on galoshes what with the dashing in and out.

"Pour it slow while I try to get some pressure." Sally poured the boiling water as slowly as she could, aiming it for the pipe that brought water up from the ground. John pumped vigorously, listening for the "wheezing" sound and the feel of heaviness, but the handle just flopped noisily up and down and no water came out. The floor was fast becoming a skating rink, except the few feet directly around the stove. Then John discovered that the pipe had burst. He would have to replace it, and this time he would have to make sure that it was wrapped securely with straw and rags as well as being boxed in with lumber.

John answered the knock, shirt-sleeved, mop in hand, and still wearing his galoshes. He apologized profusely, but the company didn't seem to mind at all. They thoroughly enjoyed the meal, sat back and talked for the rest of the afternoon, and asked to take some food home.

The talk centered around the conditions in the neighborhood. No one seemed interested or cared about what "They" were doing in Washington, nor, for that matter, in downtown Detroit's City Hall.

"We ought to put on a drive to get people to buy up these vacant lots. Then we would have power enough to DEMAND the things we need."

"Yes, we could become a fifth class city. . . ."

"We can't wait that long. What we should do is go into the city (become annexed), and as a part of Detroit, we would get water, lights, and schools — and all the things the city provides through the tax money.

Basically, these were the two opposing viewpoints that became hot issues, resolved only after petitions to go into the city had been circulated.

One day Mrs. Huggins, a slight woman with graying hair, stopped at the Parker's house.

"I have a petition, Mrs. Parker. Would you care to read it, or may I read it to yon?" Mrs. Huggins spoke perfect English and possessed a great deal of finesse.

"Read it, please, Mrs. Huggins — but if it's the one about going in the city, I'm in favor. Let me call my husband." John came in from the garden and the petition was signed.

"Thank you. I am having very little trouble — we may get a hundred percent," beamed Mrs. Huggins. John reminded her of the meeting when the argument had been presented point by point. "I think the three strongest points were transportation, schools, and the chance to have inside toilets."

"Specially the last point," Lizzie added.

"I believe you're right. Mrs. Huggins paused. "Mrs. Boyd was saying the hard part will be getting the 1200 signatures from the citizens of Detroit, indicating their willingness to accept us."

"What will all this cost us?" Lizzie asked.

"The attorney's fee is $500, and the cost of filing all petitions in triplicate is $700 . . . a total of $1200," Mrs. Huggins answered. "And I had better get on my way — we've got a deadline to meet!" She said "Goodby" and left.

Having completed the eighth grade at Carstens School on January 31, 1924, Sally entered high school. In November of that year, the voters accepted the annexation of the Eight Mile Road community, establishing Eight Mile Road as the city limits on the north (Base Line Road). All but two families had signed the petition to have the area — bounded by Greenlawn on the east, Pembroke on the south, and Birwood on the west — become a part of the city of Detroit. Now everyone waited impatiently for the improvements.

Time went forward on a sled pulled by a tropical snail. The water department said that it would pipe water into the area, but only if $30 for each of the thirteen streets was paid, representing an additional $390.

At this time, there was an average of three families living on each street. Sidewalks were finally laid, but gas and street paving came much later, when there were residents to pay for their forty-foot frontages. Fried fish, chicken dinners, barbecued ribs, and homemade cakes, pies, and ice cream were available in abundance to help defray these costs.

Sally was uncomfortable in unfamiliar surroundings. In plain language, she was afraid as she inched along in line to get enrolled in high school. She was not sure what was expected of her, and no one had given her a hint of what it would be like.

After she had been sent back for the second time to get all the papers she needed, the girl handed her a "program." She saw a group of students looking at a large board with hours, subjects, and teachers' names on it. Unobtrusively watching the others, Sally began to realize that she would have to fill in the subjects she wanted to take, only to be told that she couldn't take them.

A girl walked over and looked at her program. "They're not going to let you take those college prep courses," she said.

"What do you mean?" Sally asked, hoping not to sound as stupid as she felt.

"All the colored kids are expected to take business or domestic courses, you know — typing, shorthand or home ec."

"Why?"

"That's what you're supposed to do when you get out — be a secretary or a housekeeper."

"Is that what you want to do?"

"No, I'm going to college. That's why I'm not going to this school. I though I'd hang around to see if ANY colored kids got in, and so far, only Dr. Shelton's daughter was accepted that I know of."

Sally's program was OK'd:

English I, Typing I, Shorthand I, Gym, Lunch, and Bookkeeping I.

Mrs. Davis, whom Lizzie remembered as the one who had founded the little Mission, was interested in Sally's enrollment.

"Don't let them choose for you. You see to it that Sally takes the courses that will allow her to go on to college if she wants to. I had to speak up for my daughter, Mary."

Lizzie spoke up, still stammering, but getting the message over to the superintendent of the Detroit Public System, Mr. Frank Cody. Sally's program was changed to college prep.

ADA DIES

Things were happening in Washington, D. C., and John tried to keep up with them in the papers.

"Harding is having trouble with his cabinet, and it seems. . . ."

"That's too bad. If you don't get down to Worthy's store and bring back some kerosene, we'll be in the dark tonight," Lizzie responded.

"I thought by now we'd have electricity, at least," John grumbled, as he prepared to leave.

"Stop by and ask the coal man to bring us a couple bushels of coal." Lizzie tried to remember everything she needed. Walking to the tiny shopping area at Eight Mile was not easy in any kind of weather, especially the coming back.

September came and the A.M.E. Michigan Annual Conference convened. Reverend Marshall Pearson presented his Mission for acceptance as a recognized body, meeting the requirements of the African Methodist Episcopal Church. The name "St. Luke" was changed, because there was already a church in Highland Park with that name, so Reverend Pearson chose "Oak Grove" instead. The little structure was surrounded by oak trees; he had helped to build this wooden building. Posterity would see it develop into a $400,000 edifice.

The residents braced for another hard winter of ice-covered surfaces. Now that Sally was back home, she noticed her mother spending a lot of time over at Ada's house. On wash day, Lizzie would bring Ada's clothes over and she and Sally would wash them, too.

A large fire would be built in the heater and the kitchen stove. Clothes lines would be stretched back and forth in the living room, dining room, and kitchen to dry the clothes during the night. The next morning, the window panes would have a half-inch thickness of ice on them from dampness.

Snow fell and lay undisturbed; the moonlight created a spectacular scene. It looked as if a careless king had strewn tons of fabulous diamonds over the landscape. On Saturday nights, when the weather was bitter, John would wind the clock and set the alarm for six. This would give him time to get dressed, get a few scuttles of coal from the bin, go to Oak Grove, and make a fire. By the time the children came for Sunday School, the church would be warm.

Lizzie gave up telling him that they couldn't afford it . . . that some of the other officers should do it sometimes. But she gave vent to her feelings when John asked, "Lizzie, Rev. needs a white shirt tomorrow. He used his last one at a meeting, Friday. Would you mind doing one of mine up for him?"

"Yes, I would mind . . . if he just wore it once, he can. . . ."

John interrupted. "Tomorrow is the first Sunday. It's Communion."

"And there ain't NOBODY else in Oak Grove who has a white shirt to loan him but you!"

Marshall was Lizzie's brother-in-law, but she saw no reason to bend over backwards for him and she said so in a few thousand words. However, the shirt was prepared for John to take next door.

Christmas was celebrated by exchanging direly-needed items as gifts. Afterwards, people went back to the business of trying to endure the severe winter.

It wasn't just to give her time for studying that Lizzie kept Sally away from Ada's house as much as possible. Sally suspected a far more serious reason as she lay awake listening to the coughing all during the night. In February, Ada was no better.

"You want to take Ada's supper over? I'll be on in a minute."

Sally took the tray from her mother and started out. "Aunt Ada is all right, isn't she?"

"Sure, she's doing pretty fair."

114

Sally was thoughtful as she walked the few steps to Ada's door.

"Aunt Ada," she called.

"I'm in here . . . got a little tired and laid down. Just set it down. Where's Sister?"

Sally was in the bedroom, getting the little table and pushing it against the bed.

"I told Sister to keep you away from . . ."

Sally was taking the bowl of soup off the tray when Ada was seized with a fit of coughing and started waving Sally away.

"Thank . . . Go now . . . LEAVE!"

Ada was so upset by her being there that Sally began backing away, and her eyes filled. Lizzie was at the door as Sally reached it on her way out.

"She doesn't want me in there."

"You can stay if you want to," Lizzie told Sally and the two of them went in.

It had been understood for some time that Ada would only have contact with Lizzie. Even Marshall had to agree to this arrangement. Of course, Sally was told.

Late that night, Ada went to sleep . . . permanently.

Lizzie, the strong one, showed signs of weakening at Ada's passing. She felt so alone. After the funeral, Ada was laid to rest at Twelve Mile Road and Woodward. Lizzie lost weight and became meditative. She found comfort in a closer relationship with God.

John was reading his paper with relish. He looked up and smiled at Lizzie. "The U. N. I. A. is a powerful organization," he said, "Garvey's legionnaires lifted a streetcar off the tracks."

"What?" asked Lizzie, "Where? You mean one of those little one-man cars?"

"Must'a been one of those. It was right down there near the hall. They were having a short ceremony to escort Marcus Garvey into the hall and the motorman kept stomping on the bell. The captain told him to wait for about two minutes and they would clear the street, but the motorman didn't want to wait."

"Two minutes," Lizzie snorted. "Huh!, I waited almost an hour for that Myrtle car . . . he could'a waited ten minutes and it wouldn't make that much difference. So what did they do?"

"The captain ordered a platoon to stop the car when the motorman started to drive it into the crowd. The soldiers got around it, four in each side, and lifted it up. The motorman started screaming and they put it down and told him to wait until the people cleared the street. He waited."

John was imbued with the spirit of the Universal Nergo Improvement Association and fascinated by Marcus Garvey. Lizzie and Sally went with John to some of the meetings and were caught up in the fiery speeches and the feeling of strength and unity symbolized by the Red, Black, and Green.

Two years after Ada's death, Lizzie experienced the strangest feeling she had ever known.

"I don't know how to explain it, Reverend Lewis; I just can't put it in words." She was talking to Reverend Lewis, a neighbor and Baptist minister known as "Praying Lewis."

"Well, Sister Parker, why don't we try praying and asking God for an answer?"

"I was hoping you would say that. Could we get together sometime, anytime, soon? I don't know how long I can stand up under this feeling . . . like I'm burdened, and lonely . . . I can't keep from crying. . . ." Lizzie brushed the tears from her face. "I can't explain it. . . ."

Reverend Lewis noticed there was something different about Lizzie Parker. He couldn't pinpoint it . . . but something was different. Later, he was to recall that it was the fact that this was the first time he had heard her talk without some hesitating or stammering. She confided in Elder Miller who also suggested a special prayer service.

Lizzie, Reverend Lewis, Elder Miller, and an officer of Oak Grove met at sunrise one Sunday morning in the summer of 1927 for an unusual prayer service.

"When we got up from our knees," Elder Miller said, "there was no doubt in my mind that she had been annointed to carry the gospel."

116

"I'll remember that prayer meeting as long as I live. It was something you witness once in a lifetime," was the way Reverend Lewis summed it up.

The next year, when the Michigan Annual Conference met in the city of Grand Rapids, Bishop A. J. Carey presiding, Lizzie was given her evangelist's license, and she began a mission that would eventually take her through sixteen states and Canada.

JOHN GETS A JOB

Statistically, the community was growing — solidly black. They were taken by surprise to note that the areas east of Greenlawn and south of Pembroke were being cleared. Houses were being built there and occupied — solidly white.

The city, true to its obligation, undertook the duty of providing a school. Construction was begun at the mouth of Wisconsin (formerly Lockport), just south of Pembroke. A huge hole was dug and later abandoned. No reason was given. The hole was found to have sand that could be used commercially. It was filled with water and a child lost his life in it. Much of the sand was sold. Then the hole was used as a garbage dump.

The next site chosen was Roselawn, just north of Pembroke. Another hole was dug and abandoned and another child drowned in the water-filled excavation.

Mr. Pickens, a former school board member for the county, shook his head, "I expected Detroit to handle this school situation better than this." He was not alone. Most of the residents, and those with children, especially, wondered what it was all about.

Sally saw Lizzie coming slowly up the road and quickly laid aside the math book she had been puzzling over. She knew that she couldn't possibly get the fire going in that stubborn old range in time to convince her mother that she had started dinner at a quarter-to-five. Still, she raced outside to get kindling, rushed back, crushed and twisted some paper, grabbed some potatoes out of a bag, and reached for a knife — all in one frantic movement. But of course it was too late.

Lizzie came tiredly up the three steps and sprawled in a chair. Sally sensed that something was wrong but kept busy in the kitchen. She wished the darn fire wouldn't pop so loud, giving evidence that it had just been made and was just beginning to burn.

"No use hurryin' now; I'm too tired to eat anyway. Take your time," said Lizzie as she raised herself out of the chair. "I'm going to lay down for awhile."

Sally felt guilty. "I'm sorry, Mama. I was trying to work those problems before I forgot what the teacher said, and the time just went."

Lizzie didn't answer, and the lack of a sharp reprimand stung deeper, because Sally had no defense. She also recognized an attitude of defeatism in her mother which shook the fiber of her fragile security. She wanted to know what the trouble was, and at the same time, was frightened at the prospect of knowing. "It has to be something pretty big to shake Mama like this," Sally thought.

The matter was not discussed until a few days later when Lizzie was talking to Mrs. Wilson on the phone.

"Last Thursday, I left here right after Sally left, about 6:15. I had told Mrs. Staples that I wanted to take off about an hour and a half to take care of some business. So I went to this bank where we had made application for a loan to see about it. Child! You wouldn't believe the foolishness those people talked! What kind of house do you have? Is it brick? Is it over five years old? Do you have a full basement? Do you have at least five thousand dollars in a bank account? . . . Yes, they did! I was sick. I drug in here and went to bed. I never had anything to hit me so hard since I lost my sister. I told them we wanted the money to modernize our house. If it was brick with a full basement, or if we had five thousand dollars of our own, what would we need with a loan? It don't make sense."

The conversation went on at length. Evidently Mrs. Wilson had made a request for a loan, too, and awaited the outcome.

118

The city condemned three small houses on Wisconsin Ave. just north of Chippewa and began the third school construction. Higginbotham School was ready for occupancy in 1927. They then erected the Louis Pasteur School on Monica, just south of Pembroke. It was beginning to appear that 7½ Mile Road, later named Pembroke, was serving for more than just a street to drive on.

1927 . . . Coolidge did not choose to run!

Sally, having had three years of high school, did not plan to return. She had grown more and more dissatisfied and had retained less and less confidence. There were annoying things, like the teacher who insisted upon calling her "Sarah," and when Sally had attempted to correct her, she had said, " 'Sally' is a simple nickname for 'Sarah.' Any intelligent person knows that." On the days that Sally refused to answer to "Sarah," she was marked absent.

The main thorn in Sally's side, however, was the algebra teacher. "My name is *MISS* Kanouse." She picked up a piece of chalk, wrapped it with a piece of paper, and wrote her name on the board. The wrapping was a daily ritual. During the time when classes changed, students smiled and exchanged greetings with teachers — all but Miss Kanouse. She stood, head erect, gazing at a distant spot on a blank wall, with deilcate lace on a snow-white blouse and ankle-length black skirt revealing black silk stockings and black high-heeled shoes.

Aloof and bored, and making no effort to conceal this fact, Miss Kanouse would explain a new concept once and give an assignment, take her seat like a queen ascending a throne, and remain there until the bell rang. She then would take her place at the door, seeing no-one, saying nothing.

The sight of the algebra teacher froze Sally's mentality. Math I was hard for Sally; math she had been taught by a student, but she had been lucky to have a patient teacher for Math II, who didn't seem to mind explaining the work a second time if she was asked.

About halfway through the semester, Miss Kanouse changed. She no longer sat silently waiting for the bell to ring but whizzed through the homework until she came to Sally's paper.

119

"Miss Parker, please stand. How much time did you give to the preparation of your assignment?

"I'm not sure, but I think it was about three hours."

"Three hours — to get four correct answers out of ten?" Sally would slide back into her seat, feeling like the idiot that Miss Kanouse had announced her to be.

On other days: "Miss Parker, go to the board; take problem number 3, page 158, explain your answer."

On her feet, every problem appeared to Sally to be as clear as finding an answer to: "A has 4 cats, B has 6 chairs. If C sits on one of the chairs owned by A, how many cats will fight on Tuesday?"

Some of the students felt sorry for Sally and tried to whisper the answer or help her in some way. Whereupon Miss Kanouse would whack her desk sharply with a ruler.

"Miss Parker, I can't understand how you got in this class. You simply do not belong here."

Just before the class ended one day, Sally took her courage in hand, got out of her seat, and walked to the desk.

"Miss Kanouse, if you have a vacant period, may I come to you and get some help?" Sally asked quietly.

"Miss Parker," the teacher shouted, "If you are too dumb to get the work in class, I certainly have no time to waste on you!"

The class was startled. Sally went back to her seat, head bowed and humiliated. She tilted her head back to keep the tears from spilling out. "I'll never pass algebra under Miss Kanouse — I'm not going to pass anyway, and I DON'T GIVE A DARN!!! . . . I'm never coming back," Sally said to herself. She had enough credits to pass to the 12B but she didn't care anymore. "My mind is made up, I'm NOT coming back."

Somewhere in the back of her mind, the voice of her mother was saying, "She's doing pretty well. I'll be a proud woman when she graduates. First in the family to have a diploma to hang on the wall! I'll be a proud woman. . . ."

"Doggone it! She doesn't know what it's like. She doesn't have to take the insults and be called 'DUMB.' I don't care. I'm not coming back."

120

Sally cleared out her locker and walked out of the building, her mind recounting all the unhappy things she had borne: There had been a teacher who had told a student to teach the class for her, and there had been another one who had called on the same three people to recite every day. They were poor students and gave hilarious answers. Sally had failed because the teacher had had no recitation marks for her in the record book. A history teacher had disagreed with the textbook and had spent the whole semester pointing out the errors, but she had given a final exam on the book's information . . . and now Miss Kanouse. Enough is enough!

"What will Mama say? When do you plan to tell her?" A tiny piece of the resolve crumbled.

On the way home, Sally made plans. She would get a job, buy herself some clothes, and if Mama became too difficult, she would marry somebody. There were quite a few young people who had made the Parker house an habitual place to go and have fun on Sunday afternoons. At least two of the fellows had asked Sally to consider marriage, and if it came right down to it, she would marry one of them rather than go back to school.

John had been out since 4:30, long before daylight, standing in first one line, then another, waiting to see the card "NO HELP WANTED," then going on to the next foundry and the next — making the rounds. About eight o'clock, he would try construction. They always had as many common laborers as they needed.

"Can you handle the machines? Got your union card to lay bricks?"

John didn't bother to answer questions like these. He turned on his heels and walked away. Everybody knew black men were not permitted to train for these jobs. The unions did not allow black apprenticeship. Coolidge was catering to the big business man, and nobody anywhere cared a "fig" about the poor.

He took his time going home despite being tired, hungry, and angry. What did a man do in the house, watch his wife wash and iron or patch? Listen to her questions and try to figure a way to answer without putting himself in a bad light?

"You find anything?"

"No."

"Where did you go?"

"Usual places."

"Why do you keep going back to the same places all the time?"

"I have to go to the same places — I've been to them all!"

"Oh — you don't have to yell."

"I wasn't yelling!" John could feel the anger welling up inside and recognized the old helplessness. He was never able to sort out all the reasons for his answer, but Lizzie always seemed to trigger his outbursts. He hated these arguments, but they had almost become a way of life for them.

Deep down, he felt it was mostly his fault somehow. Acknowledging this, even to himself, made him more angry. He made a cup of tea and got something to eat. Lizzie continued to patch the hole in his overalls.

"She could have offered to fix the food," John thought.

"Hello, everybody," Sally said, forcing a cheerfulness and feeling the splintering and crackling of emotions in the quiet room.

"How do you feel, Mama? . . . Papa, I don't see you very much these days."

John explained the amount of time he spent looking for work. He was glad to have the chance to go into details for a sympathetic listener. Lizzie could hear and maybe understand how he felt.

Sally did understand. "All you can do is try, Papa. Sometimes you just can't succeed." She went to her room to change.

"I want you to get a piece of paper and a pen and write something, Sally," Lizzie said, putting her sewing away.

"All I can do is pay the interest on the lot and buy a few groceries with the money I get. I got two regular days and one every other Wednesday. Running around looking in these foremen's faces don't mean nothing. I want you to write a letter to Henry Ford and mail it to his house! Take your time, and just tell him your daddy has got to have a job . . . Go on, get busy with that letter."

Sally was surprised; she forgot all about her dilemma. Consulting the dictionary, tearing up pages of paper and starting

122

again and again . . . the letter was finally completed. She looked in the telephone directory for an address; there was none. She called a number and was told how and where to address the letter.

John sat in stony silence all during the writing and calling for information. Who ever heard of writing to Henry Ford? It's crazy! Yet it just might work, but why did Lizzie and the kid try to tell him what to do? When were they going to realize that he was the man of the house?

"You sign it," Lizzie said to Sally, "and if you don't hear from it, all you lost is a little time and a 3¢ stamp."

Sally found a job cleaning up an apartment for a doctor and his wife. The apartment building was located on the corner of Second Avenue and Euclid. She rarely had to ride the streetcar to get home. Her friend in the Studebaker was usually waiting for her.

About two weeks had passed since she had mailed the letter. As she walked in ·from her job, Lizzie, wreathed in smiles, waved a business envelope at Sally.

"They answered! He has gone to work on the midnight shift as a sweeper!!" Sally and Lizzie did a little jig.

Time after time, Sally prepared a speech to tell her mother that she would not be going back to school, but was thwarted by remarks like: "Now that your Daddy is working, you can go right on to college without having to stop and work awhile," or "You ought to make up your mind about what you're gonna take in college." Then sometimes Lizzie would ask, "Where will you be going? Don't you have to fill out papers?"

So summer glided along, heading for fall. Sally continued to work and so did John. Ford phased out the "Model T" and introduced the "Model A." The company moved from Manchester Street in Highland Park to River Rouge (Dearborn).

BE IT EVER SO TUMBLED

Lizzie stood up for a moment to rest. She bent over a large kettle filled with green beans to see if they were cooked enough. Just as she turned to inspect her jars . . . .

"Mrs. Parker!" The voice demanded attention. Mrs. Wilson was standing on the porch. Her face was wet and her percale dress was wilted with perspiration. Lizzie laid her dish cloth down, wiped her hands, and hurried to the door.

"Come in, how are you? Hot, isn't it?" Mrs. Wilson came in.

"More than just the weather," she said, as she plumped down and fanned herself with a letter. "You know, Mrs. Parker, we've been saying something's fishy in this loan business. Here is the latest," indicating the letter. "Do you realize this is the seventh bank that has turned us down? Mind you, we got good credit. Just finished paying for the car and the refrigerator — added on a couple of bicycles for the boys, paid it ALL off, but this lousy bank turns us down for a measly $500 to start modernizing the house! Imagine that! I'm so mad, I could swear."

"HUSH!" Lizzie said in astonishment. (This was not a command to cease speaking; it expressed how astonished she was at what Mrs. Wilson had told her.) "Something's GOT to be wrong," Lizzie continued. "Let's see, there's you, and the Whites, the Lorings, the Snyders, the Johnsons, the Thompsons, the Allens — how many does that make?"

"Don't forget to count yourself," reminded Mrs. Wilson, "and the Desmonds, too — that's about nine families. There's prob'ly more. People don't want to talk about being turned down by a bank, you know."

"It's the truth," Lizzie agreed. "You know, if we called a meeting to talk about this loan situation, we may be able to get all the facts from everybody who tried . . . ."

Mrs. Wilson had just thought of something so exciting that she couldn't wait for Lizzie to finish her statement. "Listen! My sister works in Birmingham, or, no, it's Bloomfield Hills. She called me the other night and said she had found a book on the place and she is going to sneak it out for us to see.

She said not to tell anybody about it but the people she was sure were with us. She'll be home this afternoon. She works half-day today and goes back tomorrow in time to serve dinner. She wouldn't tell me what it was, but she said it's SMOKING!"

"SMOKING, huh, ? . . . Well, we'll get together tonight and see what it's all about. Where do you want to meet?" Lizzie asked in a tense voice.

"People are used to coming here — your place is fine."

"That'll be fine. I'll finish canning these beans, have dinner early, and be ready. Just the regulars," Lizzie warned.

Mrs. Wilson was at the door, but she retraced her steps. She couldn't resist peeking in the kitchen. "You raise all these beans, or did you get some off the vegetable wagon?"

"We raised all of them. You remember my husband had a lot of time on his hands during planting season. After he made the rounds looking for a job, he'd come back and go out in the garden."

"They're certainly nice. I love 'Kentucky Wonders' — You be sure that you don't have company tonight. I don't want my sister to get into trouble."

"Tell everybody to get here at 7:00, as soon as it's dark. We'll close the house, pull the shades, and read by candlelight. Anybody knocking on the door — nobody here but us chickens."

"What y'all chickens doin'?" asked Laura Wilson, sharing in the joke.

"Cookin' up a plan to keep out da pot," answered Lizzie and the two women laughed. Mrs. Wilson went on down the street and Lizzie hurried back to her canning.

That night, Jesse Snyder, Winn Loring, the Wilsons, and Mrs. White walked in briskly within minutes of each other. Although the weather was warm and humid, Lizzie closed the door and windows. When it was dark, the shades were lowered. Mrs. Wilson took something that looked like a thirty- or forty-page magazine from her purse. Everybody crowded around the table to examine the document. The candlelight made reading a bit difficult, but it was easy to recognize the pictures of the homes of neighbors and the captions under the pictures.

125

"THAT'S OUR HOUSE!!" Lizzie shouted, and every mouth went "Sh-h-h-h." A small tar paper-covered house sat with an unfinished porch in the shadow of a pear tree. A walk divided a garden which stopped at the sidewalk. Under the picture was the simple statement "ANOTHER TAR PAPER SHACK."

Time had not dulled the memory of Lizzie answering the knock at the door to find two smiling ladies who asked, "Are you interested in having your property improved?"

"What a question. Of course we want to improve it. Our trouble is, we don't have any money and can't borrow any."

"We understand. That's why we have been sent to help you. Just precisely what do you want done?"

Lizzie recalled how she gave them a tour of the five small rooms and a detailed explanation of what could be done to make them livable IF money was not available to build a completely new house on the front of the lot. . . . Now here was the picture in this book, whose title was *Shacktown — Be It Ever So Tumbled.*

The little knot of intense faces looked forbidding in the dimly-lit room. Time and again they reminded each other to whisper as page after page revealed half-truths and deceptions.

"Look at old man Kenington!" There he was in baggy, dirty pants, replete with dirty undershirt. Beneath the picture, his kids and house serving as a back-drop, were these words: "THIS MAN HASN'T WORKED IN TEN YEARS. HE SAYS, 'I CAIN'T WUK NO MO, MAH BACK DONE BEEN HUIOT.' (However, he manages to father a child every year for the past six years)." The group didn't think much of old man Kenington and found it funny at first. Then, in a few minutes, they began speaking soberly.

Mr. Wilson remembered, "He didn't sign the petition to go into the city. Naturally, he doesn't care how his place looks."

Mr. Snyder added, "He wanted a farm to keep his kids busy. The city was the last thing he wanted to think about."

"They're using him and others like him to beat us over the head," Lizzie said thoughtfully, "You know what I mean?"

Winn Loring certainly did know. He took his large cigar from his mouth and leaned forward, looking over his glasses,

"This thing's gotta be handled careful. We can't lose time." He looked around at the group and pointed to the book, "That thing is dynamite!!"

Jesse Snyder, a World War I veteran with a low boiling point, wanted to know, "Who wrote this mess?" You got the feeling that if Snyder could find the writer while he was in this frame of mind, somebody would end up in the hospital, and it was unlikely to be Snyder.

"What do you do when you see something like this in black and white — in the hands of people who live in one of the richest communities in the state? How can we fight back, a handful of black folks trying to hang on to a dream?" Mrs. White asked, near to tears.

Her question filled the minds of the people in the room like an unleashed fog. Mrs. Desmond picked up the booklet and read the last paragraph again:

> "It is suggested that the shacks be demolished, salvaging as much lumber as possible, and barracks built in Inkster to house the residents. The land can then be re-subdivided into fifty frontage lots, and homes built in the thirty to forty thousand dollar bracket, thus creating an additional million dollars in taxes for the city."

When she had finished reading, a sense of helplessness hovered over the room.

"Where is your daughter?" asked Mrs. Desmond, trying to break the mood of doom.

"She's working. The doctor and his wife are always having company and it keeps her late. She's going to graduate next June, you know," and Lizzie felt better already, just thinking about the graduation.

Laura tucked the booklet into her purse, sighed heavily, and started for the door. "I think I feel worse now that I know."

"It's tough, but we are better off to KNOW what they got in mind. Now we can make our own plans." Loring was relighting his battered cigar. "Thank you, Miz Wilson, for letting us in on what's going on. As I said before, we can make our plans to fight it."

They left as quietly as they had come, each with a firm grip on his courage and with the determination to tackle this obstacle, unaware that they would search for prosperity around many a corner before they found any tangible relief.

Lizzie woke John and put his dinner on the table. She told him about the meeting while she packed his lunch.

As Sally came out of the doctor's apartment, she heard a motor start. The Studebaker backed up and the door swung open. She got in.

"Have a hard day?"

"Not too bad, just another couple for dinner. I got a little peeved when Mrs. Jennings took credit for making the lemon pie."

"Let's go around the island to cool off. When you start making pies for me, I'll be glad to give you all the credit in the world."

"Oh, fertilize!" thought Sally. She didn't want to talk about it.

The car headed down Woodward to Jefferson and east to the Belle Isle bridge. Harry slowed down to a fifteen-mile-per-hour cruise.

"I'm still waiting for your answer. My sister is making plans for early in October."

"That's nice. It will be pleasant that time of year."

"What about us?"

"I'm still trying to think. You know, getting married is . . . well, it's not like giving a party. Planning and having showers and all is a lot of fun I suppose, but figuring out how to get along for a whole lifetime . . . is something to think about."

"You've been thinking about it for months. Other people seem to make out all right; what makes you think we would have any trouble?"

Sally didn't answer, but many things were going through her mind. First of all, Harry was very popular. A lot of girls and women were interested in him and he liked his popularity. And secondly, she didn't see any future in marrying anybody and settling down to having babies and arguing.

Sally tried to choose her words carefully, because she knew

that in spite of her real feelings, she might have to resort to marrying Harry rather than face Miss Kanouse again.

"Maybe if we really tried . . . maybe . . . ."

Marshall was alone now, and he read everything he could get his hands on to help pass the time. One day an advertisement caught his attention, and he went next door to show it to John.

"Brother Parker, I've got something here that sounds mighty good." He pointed to the corner of the little publication. John adjusted his glasses and read it. The two men looked at each other and a broad smile spread over the faces of both men.

"The JANTHA PLANTATION has hundreds of acres of bananas. They need money to buy equipment to speed up delivery and sales. Shares are offered at ten dollars a share, as long as they last — GUARANTEED to bring dividends within six months!"

John and Marshall invested. Marshall dreamed of a fine church to pastor; John dreamed of his beautiful permanent home, built by professional carpenters on the front of his lot.

After a year and a half, Jantha Plantation was still needing money to buy equipment and no dividends had yet been declared. But a bulky letter from Colorado offered John another "opportunity." It told of a newly-discovered vein in an old gold mine. Only a selected few special people were being notified about a limited amount of stock. Big companies had bought most of it, but if he hurried . . . . John invested.

The second letter that came asking for additional money to get gilt-edged bonds was questioned by Lizzie. "Why do they want to be so good to you? Don't you know that anything that was actually going to make any money would be bought up so fast by big business men, you wouldn't even smell it. Instead of wasting that money, you ought to be saving to have a basement dug and move this house up over it."

John winced at the mere mention of such a thing.

Lizzie could read a little better now that she had attended evening school. It was important, because the community was organized now and meetings were being held regularly. Because of the nature of the business transacted and the existing situation, it was necessary to be able to read.

When the class had ended, the instructor had reminded the students that the only way it would be continued was if at least twenty people were to enroll in the next class. It was now past the middle of August, and Lizzie started going from house to house, telling her friends and neighbors about the class and inviting them to make plans to enroll.

While visiting a neighbor and talking about evening school, she was jokingly asked, "How are you going to manage your lessons while planning your daughter's wedding?"

"I won't have to think about that for quite a while. She will be in shcool until next June, and then I hope she can go on to college."

"That's not the way I heard it," the neighbor said and waved.

When the third person asked about the upcoming wedding, Lizzie was disturbed and a little angry. She told herself that it was silly and a lot of gossip, but she meant to look into the matter.

When Sally came home that evening, Lizzie confronted her with the question, "What's this I hear about you marrying this guy Harry?"

"Well . . . I didn't say for sure."

Lizzie continued, "I understand there will be a double wedding, you and Harry and his sister and the fellow she's going with."

Sally got a mental picture of actually standing in church and saying "I do" to Harry, and it was too much.

"I'm just not going back to school, Mama!" Sally blurted out and began to cry.

"WHY?" Lizzie's eyes searched her child for explanations: Why was she crying? Why didn't she want to go back to school? What had happened to give this timid girl courage to take a decisive stand like this?

"Why did you say you would marry him?"

"I didn't say I WOULD, I only said 'MAYBE.' "

"It's all over the neighborhood about your marrying him. Why didn't you say something to me about it?"

130

Sally then told her mother the real reason that she had given any thought to marriage. Lizzie listened as she told about the experiences she had had with some of the teachers, and how she had decided not to go back after the episode with Miss Kanouse.

"Other teachers would announce to the class where they could be reached during their vacant periods, in case anyone wanted extra help, so I thought it would be all right to ask . . ."

Lizzie was silent for a while, then she said, "I . . . also . . . am going to-to-to the super-in-tendent and also . . . find out . . . also why she can . . . treat kids like that." She was stammering terribly. She was angry. Her mind went back to the kicking incident at Moore School. She had to go to the Board of Education now because she had worked too hard to build a speck of confidence in Sally to allow it to be destroyed by a thoughtless person who called her "dumb."

September came and Sally went back to school. There was no double wedding that involved the Parker family.

Four years later, a young man came along who fitted Sally's idea of a husband. A mutual love culminated in marriage.

WELFARE

Eight Mile was growing. Its counterpart, Ferndale, was also growing. Baseline Road separated the two communities but they had many things in common: No uniform housing regulations, muddy roads waiting to become streets, and a long walk for everybody to get the bus, which terminated at Wyoming and Eight Mile Road.

The shopping area now included the Lett Store, a pool hall, Doc Washington's Drug Store, Jim Dolan's Market, and Alfred Davis' Funeral Home, as well as Worthy's Store.

The struggle continued unabated for permanent housing. The name "Hoover" was a bad word. Soup lines were getting longer.

131

Lizzie looked out to see a new model "A" Ford roll up. The young white driver helped John out. John's pants leg was rolled up and his leg was bandaged.

"He's been to the hospital, Mrs. Parker, and the doctor wants to see him day after tomorrow. Someone will be here to take him. No broken bones, but a pretty bad bruise and a cut. He is being taken care of by some very good doctors."

"I slipped in a grease spot and fell," John explained, "Slid into a machine. I have some pills to take when the pain gets bad." Lizzie helped him into the house.

"I don't want to go to bed, at least for awhile; I feel pretty good right now." John sat down and gazed out of the window. What do you talk about? What do you say? This was terrible; it was like he and Lizzie were strangers. He wished the kid were here.

"What would you like for your dinner?" Lizzie asked, and realized that it was a stupid question the minute it was out of her mouth. Every penny she could scrape together had been used to buy cement block to build a basement for their house. For dinner there was a pot of neck bones cooked until the meat fell off the bones, to which some wild onions had been added, and a pot of rice. Lizzie hoped John would be hungry enough to eat it.

When Sally came home, she was wide-eyed and upset about the accident. "Papa, what happened? You didn't break any bones, I hope. How do you feel?"

"I got a chance to ride in a new car, right off the assembly line," John told her. "It's a nice, roomy car. They expect to sell a lot of them."

The evening was full of evasive, nonsensical talk as John was helped to bed. The honest thoughts in each mind centered around the fact that John was 55-years-old, and the chances of his getting back on the job were slim indeed.

"We can't make it any longer — there's nothing to eat and no coal to cook it with if we had it. I'm going to the Welfare!" Lizzie announced one day.

Sally's stomach did a flip. "Oh, Lord, how degrading," she

thought, but did not protest when Lizzie said, "There will prob'ly be papers to make out — you better come with me."

Lizzie and Sally entered a large, untidy building at about 9:00. It was crowded. Each face had the forlorn look of the forsaken. A few whites were sprinkled through the crowd, sitting on chairs and rows of benches. A name would be called out and someone would get up, looking ashamed, and go into a closed-in area for questioning. At about 3:45 Lizzie's name was called.

"Are you Lizzie Parker?"

"Yes."

The worker looked up quickly and it seemed that she had expected to be answered, "Yes Ma'am."

"How long you been out of work?"

"About a month."

"You got a husband?"

"Yes." Again, the look.

"Where is he?"

"He's out looking for a job."

"Oh, really?" she laughed. "How long since he had a job?"

"He got hurt — slipped and hurt his leg on a machine at Ford's and he can't get back on the job. He's been off about five months."

"You got any money in the bank?"

"WHAT?"

"You got any money in the bank? If so, how much?"

"No."

"What did you do with your money?"

Lizzie's lips puckered and words started stumbling and halting. Sally had noted the condescending attitude of the worker and had been angry for some time.

"We can't do anything for you unless you can prove to us what you did with your money."

"Who is the . . . also supervisor?"

"Why?"

"I'm . . . also going to talk . . . also to somebody so I can . . . also get a . . . also emergency check before I . . . also leave here. There's nothing to eat at home . . . and . . . also I came here to . . . also get some food . . . I've been here . . . a-a-a-all day, and I . . . also don't intend to . . ."

"What's the trouble?" A woman had come out of one of the offices as Lizzie's voice rose.

"This woman is demanding that I give her a check! I can't give her my money unless she's willing to answer the questions!"

"YOUR money??" shouted Lizzie. "YOU . . . also got no money!! I am . . . also asking for Welfare help . . . also like everybody else in this . . . t-t-t-town who's facing starvation. It's not coming . . . also out of your pocket."

The woman from the office looked at the clock. "It's closing time, but if you will come back tomorrow, I'll take your case. Just go in that door there and I'll talk with you tomorrow. What's the name?"

"Lizzie Parker."

"I will expect you tomorrow, Mrs. Parker."

The Donahoos sent over some of their dinner for the Parkers that night, and Lizzie borrowed carfare from the Snyders and kept her appointment the next day. After talking with the supervisor, Lizzie was given an emergency check and placed on the Welfare rolls.

POLIO STRIKES

The pioneers in the community were close-knit. Some of those who came later acted as though the old-timers had grown up with the dandelions, arriving shortly after the caveman. Those pushing for permanent homes were careful about the screening of anyone allowed to take part in their planning. The ranks were small but firm. Their attention was called to the number of lots that had been lost during the long periods of unemployment. An investigation was made to ascertain the possibility of buying back some of the lots. The state land board auctioned off the lots in parcels — no bidding on single lots.

The deepening depression caused people to continue losing their land. Home seekers were getting alarmed. . . . Then came 1932! ! Franklin Delano Roosevelt was elected after campaigning to "REMEMBER THE FORGOTTEN MAN!" The disinterest and attitude of isolation where Federal Government was concerned came to an abrupt end in the Eight Mile Road community. Here was a man elected to the highest office in the land who not only said but acted like he cared about the little people.

Roosevelt was busy utilizing the alphabet to create stop-gap programs calculated to relieve the welfare rolls.

Sally said "I do" and became Mrs. Robert Hayward at a time when no one in his right mind would have thought of taking on additional responsibility. In spite of the fact that Bob had been laid off from his railroad porter's job, he and Sally agreed that two could starve as cheaply as one, and the Parkers made room for them.

Bob Hayward was a tall, brown-skinned fellow with a knack for telling tales, tales that his friends had heard dozens of times but asked to hear again and again. He was not all "fun and laughter," though. He understood that, although he was without a permanent job, he would be responsible for half of the utility bills and would take care of his own family's upkeep.

One day during the summer of '34, when Bob was working as a weed cutter on the W.P.A., Sally was fixing a sandwich for him to take on the job. "Things are picking up a little now. I don't think it will be long before they call you back on the road," she said.

"It can't come too soon," Bob answered, reaching for his hat. "I'm going to need a lot more money than weed cutting brings in. You know, from the looks of the way things are shaping up, we may have two birthdays in August — I hope it's on the sixth." He grinned and winked at Sally as he rushed out. Sally didn't care what day it happened. She was tired of shuffling along, laden down, and longed to have it over with.

On September 1, 1934, a robust baby girl weighing seven pounds joined the Hayward household and became Lizzie's and John's first grandchild.

During her first year, as Enid learned to walk and talk, Japan invaded Manchuria, Mussolini started war to make Ethiopia a part of the Italian Empire, and Adolph Hitler made plans to break the Treaty of Versailles.

"Haile Selassie came to talk to the President," Sally told Bob.

She was feeding Enid and encouraging her to make her dinner "all gone" so that she could see the pretty flower in the bottom of the bowl. Every few seconds, Sally had to remove Enid's fingers from her mouth to put in the spoonful of food. The baby had formed a habit of sucking the index and middle fingers of her left hand.

"You reckon it will do any good? Ethiopia is such a small country . . . but Roosevelt is for the little people," Bob was saying. "He may give them some help."

Sally took a diaper and bound a piece of cardboard to Enid's arm, preventing her from bending it. Enid popped the fingers of her right hand into her mouth, although she soon took them out again. She was six-months-old and very persistent.

Bob turned the radio on, and he and Sally listened to the news. The President had received Selassie and had listened to his plea, but there was no word at this time about what, if anything, the United States would do. There was more news of the conquering Adolph Hitler. They talked about it for a few minutes.

"Look! Look at the Worm — what do you think of that?" laughed Bob. He had nicknamed Enid "Worm" because of the way she crawled. While the news was being broadcast, Enid had untied the diaper and pushed the cardboard around, and she now sat sucking her favorite left-hand fingers.

By 1937, Hitler had annexed Austria, swallowed Czechoslovakia, and invaded Poland. Roosevelt and Secretary Hull urged the citizens of the United States to get involved with the situation in Europe, but the majority preferred "isolation."

"What do you think about the war in Europe?", was the question often asked when people got together.

"Well, I don't know much about it, but I don't want any of my boys going anywhere to fight for people I know nothing about. Furthermore, what are we supposed to get out of it?

136

Would they come over here and fight for us? Plenty has happened to Negroes, and I don't remember anybody taking any notice of it."

"It really don't concern us . . . it's THEIR war."

Bob and Sally felt that there was no use in getting upset about something which they had nothing to do with. They didn't like the way the "colored" troops were being handled, but again, it was mostly hearsay and possibly the remnants of the caustic feelings of World War I veterans. There was so much room for misunderstanding when the only thing one could do was to vote every year or so, and then one was only taking other people's word for what the candidates stood for, none of whom were colored.

In a few months, Enid would be five, and Sally kept her eyes peeled for sales to get school clothes, looking forward to getting her in kindergarten in September.

A neighbor, Mrs. Brown, reminded Sally, "It's the middle of July; we better take the kids to a park before summer gets away."

The trip to the park had been tiring, but the weather was so hot that it had been nice to get out of the house. However, Enid still seemed extremely tired when Sally gave her a bath that evening.

"I no want it," Enid announced, and pushed the cereal away. Sally didn't insist; she and Mrs. Brown had allowed the kids to eat everything in sight all afternoon — ice cream, caramel corn, milk, and hot dogs.

"So into bed with you then," and Sally lifted Enid into her bed.

Bob was back on the road, running "extra," catching a run whenever he could. He was out on a special and would not return for three or four days.

It was late when Sally woke up. She was surprised to find Enid still in bed. "We both were exhausted," Sally thought as she yawned and stretched. Then she noticed that Enid was not asleep. She reached over and felt the child's forehead and realized that Enid had a temperature. Sally got dressed and reached for the phone.

"Oh, for heaven's sake, it's Saturday — no doctor is in his office on Saturday."

She spent the day trying to coax Enid to drink some juice or soup, with very little success. The child's listlessness disturbed Sally in spite of the fact that she reminded herself that children often got high temperatures and that it was really nothing to worry about.

On Sunday John went to church, but Sally kept watch over Enid, who remained in bed, wanting to be carried into the bathroom and put back into bed. Sally was anxious and fearful. She called Children's Hospital and was told to call a city physician. About 4:00 that afternoon, a doctor came.

"How long has she been sick?" he asked.

"She didn't feel well yesterday morning — I guess since yesterday."

He glanced at her in the crib. "Well, I'm not going to touch her, I've got kids of my own. Get her into the hospital first thing tomorrow morning." He went into the bathroom and scrubbed his hands as if he had examined her from head to toe.

John came in as the doctor was leaving.

"Papa, will you ask someone to take us to the hospital tomorrow morning? I have to take Enid — she's sick."

"What's the matter with her?"

"I don't know. The doctor just told me to take her in tomorrow."

"I'll get somebody, don't worry . . . even if we have to call a taxi."

"Wait until after you eat your dinner. I'll heat up the roast."

Lizzie was staying at her place of employment for a month. The Staples were away on vacation and needed someone to stay with an elderly aunt until they returned.

Enid did not want to walk, and Sally carried her out to the car and into the hospital. John took her while the nurse gave directions.

"She's pretty heavy. I'll follow you," John said, and they started down the long corridor, then another, turning here and there, until they reached the place to which the nurse had directed them.

They had progressed through two examinations and three doctors when one of the doctors said, "Mrs. Hayward, we don't know how bad she has it, but we know she has . . . INFANTILE PARALYSIS!" The floor dropped from under Sally's feet and she collapsed. A nurse pushed a chair under her as the doctor braced her against the door frame and eased her into the chair.

This terrifying disease would later be known as "polio," but now science was unfamiliar with it and groped for effective medication. The doctor explained that the only means of counteracting the germ known to them was spinal injection. He was reluctant to say it, but he did: "In all fairness, I have to tell you that sometimes the needle contacts a nerve, and if it does, it results in paralysis from the waist down. It is the chance we have to take."

When John and Sally returned, the house had been quarantined. Sally dully read the notice that had been tacked on the door, and she and John turned and walked away slowly. They wandered up and down the streets aimlessly for an hour or so.

"That's silly to quarantine an empty house, Papa."

"It don't make much sense. We may as well go in. We can't sleep in the street," John answered.

"Of course, once we go in, we can't come out — and no one else can come in . . . not even Bob or Mama."

"That's something to think about," said John. He halted and began searching his pockets. Sally looked in her purse and found a dollar and some change.

"Here, Papa, get whatever you can — mostly canned goods, I guess." John accepted the money and started walking toward Eight Mile Road.

The house looked strange as Sally tiptoed around, hanging up clothes and tidying things that had been left undone in their haste to get to the hospital. She thought she had better call her mother.

"Mama, I put Enid in the hospital this morning . . . She's very sick, the doctors think she has infantile paralysis." There was silence at the other end. Sally knew how shocked her mother must be and decided not to tell her about the spinal injection.

"No, nobody can visit her for at least a week. Then only Bob and I will be allowed to go. . . . He's gone to the store to get a few things. The house is under quarantine . . . Yes, Mama, I'll try," Sally answered, when told to keep her chin up. Her voice was beginning to quiver and she didn't want her mother to know that she was crying. Mothers seem to have a sixth sense that makes them aware of things their children try to conceal.

That night, after a silent meal, John sat with the evening paper still folded, gazing into space. Sally washed the dishes, cleaned the stove, and was about to wash the kitchen curtains when she heard Lizzie's voice.

"Sally! Open the window." Sally rushed to the bedroom window, which was nearest to Marshall's house next door. She and John squeezed their shoulders together and leaned out to talk to Lizzie.

"I thought I'd better come home. Mrs. Staple's sister is staying with the aunt. They're supposed to be back next week."

"I'm sure glad you're here, Mama. This is something — locked out of your own house."

"Now isn't it? Have you heard anything else since you called me?"

"No . . . , well, . . . no," said Sally. John cleared his throat.

"It's going to be hard. You see they tell you straight that they don't know much about it, and that you don't really have much of a choice . . . ."

"A choice? About what?" asked Lizzie.

John cleared his throat again. He just didn't want to come right out and say it. Sally puffed out her cheeks, blew the air out, and began, "The doctor had a long talk with me and Papa. He said what they have been doing is . . . is . . . trying to head off paralysis by putting medicine in the spine. They call it a spinal injection. The only thing, sometimes the needle may come in contact with a certain nerve, and if it does, the patient will be paralyzed from the waist down. He said it doesn't happen often, but he thought in all fairness he should tell us. They don't know any other treatment for it at this time. With no treatment, she may not get any worse, there's no way of telling, but she can't get better. . . . They might be able to teach her to walk with a brace or. . . ."

Lizzie had been listening intently. She interrupted Sally, "That's all right. I know a man."

"But, Mama, like I told you on the phone, it will be a week before anyone can visit. . . . Oh, is he a specialist?"

"He's the greatest doctor ever known."

"He may still have to have recommendations to get permission to get in. I think they are very strict about . . . ."

"He don't need to ask nobody permission. He goes in and nobody can stop him. I've talked with Him and everything's going to be all right!"

"Yes, Mama, I think I understand," Sally was crying again and she left to get a handkerchief.

"Prayer changes things," John stated. Then he asked, "Are you going to be all right over there? Reverend has been gone two weeks and I doubt there is much in the way of food in the house."

"I had something before I left the job. Just lucky I still have a key. It's kind of strange coming over here again. What did Sally fix for your dinner?"

"For a minute, I couldn't remember. We had salmon croquettes and tomatoes, and she made some lemonade . . . it was nice."

Sally returned to the window and the three continued small talk for quite awhile.

A. Phillip Randolph was scheduled to be in Detroit on Labor Day. The Detroit Local of the Brotherhood of Sleeping Car Porters was buzzing with preparations. Bob was among the staunch members. He had laid his job on the line to support the organization. A barbecue was planned to raise additional funds to carry out plans for the Labor Day affair. Bob was known for making good barbecue and the members depended on him to cook the meat.

The planning meeting had lasted until noon. By the time Bob reached home, it was in the middle of the afternoon. He was preoccupied with Randolph's visit as he opened the door and put his bag down.

"Where is the Worm? The house is unusually quiet," he thought. Then he saw Sally's face and knew there was trouble somewhere.

"What's the matter, Hon?"

"You didn't see the sign?"

"What sign?"

"We are under quarantine . . . Enid is in the hospital."

"In the hospital?" Bob was shouting. "What hospital? Why? When did you take her? What's the matter with her?" Questions tumbled out of him like a rock slide. Sally led him to the door and pointed to the piece of yellow cardboard.

"Oh, my Lord . . . Oh, my Lord!!" Bob kept saying over and over.

"I carried her in yesterday morning — Papa and I. She's in Children's Hospital. We can visit her in about a week."

Bob was too stunned to comprehend what Sally was saying.

"I'll get C. George to run me down there." He picked up his bag then put it down. Bob shook his head to clear his thinking and found himself repeating, "Oh, my Lord." Sally told him again about having to wait a few days before they could visit; this time, he accepted it.

They called daily and talked to the doctor or someone at the hospital. Permission was granted for visiting on Saturday afternoon. Sally and Bob waited in the lobby for the time to go upstairs to the ward where Enid was. Neither spoke, and they both summoned every ounce of courage that may have lurked in the furthermost repository of their beings. The elevator took them to the third floor. The nurse was cheerful as she led them down the hall and explained that the children were still in semi-isolation.

"You can visit for half an hour. The doctor will confer with you then, and by that time, you'll have just enough time to say goodbye before the visiting hour is over," she said.

They heard her high-pitched laughter before they saw her. She was having a pillow fight with the child she shared the room with. Then they saw her, bouncing off her bed and running to retrieve her pillow to throw it again. Bob and Sally stood motionless. Sally remembered her mother's voice, "I know a man . . . everything's going to be all right." Enid saw them and squealed, "Mommy! Daddy!"

"How's Daddy's little Worm?" Bob said, sweeping her up and burying his face in her mid-section while she giggled and grabbed a handful of hair.

"Put me down, I wanna show you . . ." Everything: the little patient who shared the room, each toy, the various exercises used for therapy . . . everything. Sally and Bob kept their eyes glued on her, watching every move she made, hardly daring to breathe. The nurse came and announced snack time and indicated a small office where Sally and Bob could wait to see the doctor.

He came in shortly. After introductions, he said, "Do you realize what lucky parents you are?" looking from Bob to Sally. "She is going to come through this thing with hardly a limp. I really don't think you know what that means percentage-wise." He quoted figures that seemed to indicate that Enid was part of a very microscopic group that recovered with such a small degree of crippling.

When it was time to go, Sally and Bob went back to Enid's room to say "Goodbye." She had thought she would be going home and began to cry.

"No, no, Honey, we'll come back to see you. . . ."

"I wanna go home!"

"The doctor says you can come home soon. . . ."

"I wanna go NOW with you. . . ."

The nurse began leading Bob and Sally away. She was used to the wailing of little people, but Sally and Bob were not. Gradually, the whole building was filled with the cries of children pleading to be taken home. Bob reached for his handkerchief.

"Maybe we can walk down," Sally said when she saw her husband's face. "Sometimes the elevators are so crowded." They walked a short way to the "EXIT" sign and disappeared in the stairwell, where Bob leaned against the wall and cried his heart out. Sally took his hand.

143

"Bob, she can walk!! The doctor said she won't even limp and the only trace will be a fraction of an inch difference in the size of her legs. Let's be thankful for that."

"I am thankful. I just can't stand it when she asks to come home and I can't take her."

Bob regained his control and he and Sally went home to tell the good news.

Shortly after, Enid was released. Sally enrolled her in Higginbotham's kindergarten. It was evident, and quite early, that Sally would come to know Enid's teachers well.

THE COMMUNITY IS DIVIDED

"Why don't you sit down, girl?"

"I don't know . . . I'm upset, I guess. Seems like the more we try, the less we accomplish. I really expected to hear from the last contact we made. It's been more than a week now."

"Well, standing up's not going to make anything happen."

"I think I'll call a few people." Sally started to call men who she thought may have had knowledge of the reasons for the lack of progress. Lizzie listened and asked questions about each conversation.

Serving as "spokesman" for the community kept Sally on her toes. She was anxious for results for two reasons: she was a representative of the neighborhood, and she had a personal interest in getting F.H.A. housing approval and community-approved land use.

"May I speak to Mr. Grover, please? . . . Mr. Grover, I am Mrs. Hayward, the spokesman for the West Eight Mile Improvement Association. We spoke to you a few days ago about—"

"No, Mr. Grover, there is no other committee to my knowledge but the one I am a part of . . . ."

"May I make an appointment with you to discuss this situa-

144

tion further? . . . Thank you. May I bring at least two others with me? . . . Thank you, again. We will be there."

"SO!!! THAT'S WHERE THE HIDDEN WEDGE LIES!"

"Where?" asked Lizzie.

"The chairman has been taking people down to various agencies as a committee representing the community . . . they tell a very different story than the one I am instructed to tell."

"WHAT? . . . You going to look into it, of course?"

"Yes, I made an appointment . . . I'm going to call a couple of people to go with me . . . . THAT'S NERVE!!"

Sally walked in and Lizzie read her face. She was angry.

"How did the meeting go?" she asked Sally.

"He told us the same thing he had said over the phone. I wanted him to say it before witnesses. Now, I'm going to request an emergency meeting of the steering committee." She went to the phone and talked briefly to the chairman of the Improvement Association.

"He said it would be all right to call the emergency meeting, but he was very anxious to know what the developments were that I wanted to bring to their attention."

Fortunately, only two members of the steering committee were absent. The meeting was called to order and Sally was asked to make her report:

"Mr. Chairman, I am concerned about the fact that in spite of the promises from some of the contacts we have made, no one seems to be following through. I called Mr. Grover and discussed this problem with him. He stated to me then, and later in the presence of Mrs. Williams, that another group, posing as the representatives of the community, had appeared before several agencies, including his agency, to ask a halt in the considerations I have asked for. According to the minutes of each meeting, Mr. Chairman, I have stated, to the best of my ability, exactly what the body has instructed me to say . . . ."

"Do you mean Mr. Grover of the Recreation Department?" asked the chairman.

"Yes. He asked us to request a meeting of the Association, so that he might attend and conclude for himself which committee was bona fide. While I have the floor, I move that such

145

a meeting be called and that Mr. Grover be invited to attend."

"He'll never put his foot in my meeting to try to make a fool of me," the chairman replied, and refused to present the motion.

Sally gathered up her coat and marched out of the meeting, followed by Jesse Snyder.

"Wait, Mrs. Hayward, I'm leaving, too. I'll take you home."

"Ain't that something?" Snyder said as he cranked up. "I knew he wanted to protect his job, but my God, this is too much!!"

"Mr. Snyder, the people are being double-crossed. They don't have a representative . . . I mean, having another committee asking or demanding the things that we oppose, and opposing the things that we are asking for . . . ."

"But, you see, they don't know it. The community don't know they're being sold down the river," said Snyder.

"That's true. . . . They ought to be told about it."

"Let's tell 'em!"

Lizzie was surprised when Sally and Mr. Snyder walked in. "Short meeting . . . what happened?"

They told her and sat down to draw up the wording for an announcement. Jesse Snyder laid down a $5 bill.

"Tell the printer to get 'em back to you as quick as he can." He left, saying that he had to be on the job by 5:30 the next morning.

As a result of the announcements calling for a general meeting, an overflow audience was in attendance, many of whom had never attended a meeting before and had no knowledge of the work the steering committee had undertaken, nor what was at stake.

The chairman had the advantage. He called the meeting to order and proceeded to make a tearful appeal: "I have no idea what this meeting is about, but if anyone is not satisfied with the job I am trying to do, after all the things I have done for many of you personally, I will resign."

"NO . . . NO . . . NO . . . ." came from all over the room. One lady rose, "Mr. Chairman, I don't know anything about why we was asked to come out here . . . but I won't stand for

146

no resigning." It was clear that those in the "know" were out-numbered, and that the chairman was secure in his position as head of the Improvement Association.

The next week, a meeting was called at the home of the Parkers and the regulars came and organized the Carver Progressive Club. Winn Loring was elected as its first president.

One of the first things the newly-formed club did was become a chartered organization with the State of Michigan. This was in 1940. After a year, as the by-laws provided, another president was elected, and Loring was freed to fight vigorously from the floor for housing.

THE CARVER PROGRESSIVE CLUB

The Government would guarantee repayment to any bank who loaned money for homebuilding. It was an over-simplified statement, but that's how the homeseekers in the Eight Mile area explained the Federal Housing Administration Act, and they were jubilant.

As industry absorbed the unemployed, applications were resubmitted to banks for loans. White neighborhoods now occupied areas from Greenlawn to Livernois, north and south of Pembroke. The latest development for whites began at Mendota and had progressed as far as Meyers Road.

"Homes to the east of us, homes to the south of us, homes to the west of us, but nothing for us," was the way the homeseekers summed it up.

"The minutes will stand approved. According to the minutes, we have some unfinished business. . . ."

The Carver Progressive Club was in session. Every person who had come to the Parkers and strained his eyes to read by candlelight a few years ago was a staunch member of this organization, and they meant business.

The president continued, "We will hear from the committee who investigated the wall."

"We talked with the man who is head of the developing company. He said the wall is on HIS property and there wasn't anything we could do about it. He further said that he was forced to shut off the view of our delapidated houses to increase his chances of selling those homes on Mendota. Those homes are F.H.A. approved too."

So the six-foot concrete wall remained on the line of the alley at the rear of Birwood. But the Carver Progressive Club members had been slapped in the face before, and this, though humiliating, did not faze them. (Photo of wall on p. 190)

"Mr. President."

"Mr. Loring."

"Mr. President, members. We got to seek out people with power and influence and sit down and talk with these people — get them to help us and to support the things we try to do. We ought to have something like a secret committee to look into this kind of help."

His suggestion was accepted, followed by many meetings with dozens of people: political, religious, financial, and legal. The committee worked out key questions to ask the potential benefactor.

"I have to work late tonight — Why not drop by about 9:15?" Promptly at the stated hour, three members of the secret committee would arrive and be led into a back office.

"I take this precaution so we won't be disturbed," Mr. X would say apologetically. The member asking the questions would sit nearest to him while the other two members took positions where his reactions could be watched closely.

"We are glad you had the time to see us. Are there any questions we could answer to brief you on the current situation?"

"No."

"What can you do to assist us, or do you have suggestions for a better strategy?"

If the answer was: "There is very little you can do, unless you have money for a long legal fight," or "Perhaps it would be a good idea to talk to Mr. Y; I know him personally and . . . ." (The committee knew him, too, and what he stood for), or if Mr. X brushed them off with, "I'll have to give it some

148

thought . . . ." the meeting was short. They thanked Mr. X, left, and crossed his name off the list.

The committee's efforts were not all in vain. A few helpers asked to remain anonymous, but others gave their support openly: Reverend Mr. Horace White, pastor of Plymouth Congregational Church; Vernon J. Brown, seeking the office of Lieutenant Governor of Michigan; and Mr. Joy, a member of the State Land Board.

Lizzie and Sally worked as feverishly as anyone to advance the cause of housing, as committee members, officers, or whatever. With the help of Bob, Sally's husband, a basement was dug, the house was moved up, and a few things were done to modernize it.

Meantime, John built a two-wheeled cart and collected newspapers and cardboard. This he bailed and sold. He had a load ready to sell when someone backed a truck up and stole it during the night. The next load he accumulated, Lizzie insisted upon his using the money to buy a suit at one of the leading men's stores. It was his first.

Bill Joy ran up the walk and knocked on the Parker's door. "Come in, Mr. Joy, it's good to see you. Sit down."

"I've just got a minute. I'm on my lunch break — wanted to pass this on to you. Whoever OWNS the land is going to make a lot of difference in this struggle to get F.H.A. Now we know the state has reclaimed a number of parcels through default. The board should be persuaded to side with you, rather than lease the land they own to the Public Housing Administration." Joy was prancing about and pounding his fist in his open palm as he talked.

"My God! All those vacant lots in the hands of F.P.H.A. would drown us . . . what's our move?" Lizzie asked.

"Here is a list of names and telephone numbers. Set up a meeting, the quicker the better. You know how to reach me if you need me." Joy left in a run, jumped in his car, and drove off.

Sally got busy with the list. In about two hours a day and hour had been agreed upon, and Reverend S. C. Davis had given permission to use Oak Grove Church for a July 9th meeting.

Lizzie had no doubt about getting Reverend Davis' co-operation, because he delighted in listening to politicians. At a previous meeting, in the heat of the election year, a group of office-seekers had prevailed upon the pastor and the trustees to allow them to hold a rally at the church. It had been well-attended and the rostrum had been lined with candidates. Most of them had spoken briefly and had urged the voters to support them. One candidate had prefaced his speech by saying, "I always feel at home with you people. I was raised by an old black mammy and I spent as much of my childhood in her humble shack as I spent in my own home. You people are very dear to me and if I am elected, I shall see to it that . . . etc., etc., etc."

When he had finished, Reverend Davis had stood and extended his hand, smiling, "I just had to interrupt the meeting to shake the brother's hand," he said, "We have SO much in common. You see, I was raised by an old white mammy . . . ." The congregation had roared; the candidate had remembered a pressing engagement and had not been able to remain to hear the rest of Reverend Davis' story.

July 9th!! Winn Loring and Jesse Snyder volunteered to serve as Sergeants-at-Arm. No one would get into this meeting unless he was readily identified as one who should be there.

One o'clock, and members of the State Land Board began arriving. Joy rushed in and whispered to Loring, "Surprise! The Common Council is coming!"

"The Common Council??"

"Give them a feeling for the human side of this situation," Joy said, and settled back to watch the drama.

The church was almost full. Among those present were members of the Carver Progressive Club, Council members, State Land Board members, Reverend Mr. Horace White, Reverend Davis and Vernon Brown.

Reverend Davis called the meeting to order, welcomed the visitors, and turned the meeting over to the president of the Carver Progressive Club.

"I am not good at making speeches. We are interested in our community. Many of us have tried to do more in the way of either building new houses or modernizing the ones we have. Everybody knows how we've been denied loans, but we're not giving up. Some of us have lost the lots we were trying to buy when work was slow, but we want every inch of ground in this community used for PERMANENT HOMES! We believe that our people have had enough temporary shelters. We want decent houses to live in like those houses across the wall on Mendota, and this is what we have told our spokesman, Mrs. Parkers' daughter, to say wherever she goes!"

There was applause at this point. The speaker felt that he had made the purpose of the meeting clear. He asked if there were questions and then sat down.

A member of the Common Council wanted to know if there was anyone present who had been denied a loan for home improvement, and the hands of every resident went up.

There was little else to discuss, and the meeting was used to allow members of the two visiting bodies to become acquainted. Each gave his name and where he lived. The State Land Board members had come from all over the state and wanted to have a tour of the community.

As the meeting adjourned, there was a distinct atmosphere of friendliness and Joy winked broadly. They felt that the scales had been tipped in favor of those praying for permanent homes — HALLELUJAH!!!!

FIGHT IN THE CITY COUNCIL

Cars were lined up to get into every parking lot that was within two blocks of City Hall. It was hot, even at 9:00 in the morning. As Sally and the neighbors who had come down with her got out to hurry to the meeting, the attendant asked, "What the hell is going on? I never seen so many of our folks down here this time of day."

"The Council is hearing arguments from the propositions presented by the F.H.A. and the F.P.H.A. this morning," someone said as the group rushed on.

That was the way the little notice had read in the paper, and to the casual observer this was a fair description of the proceedings. But as wave after wave of people with strained, anxious faces packed the chambers of the Council, squeezed around the walls, and spilled out into the halls, one realized that this was more than a routine hearing.

To understand how deep the emotions ran, one had to be aware of the powers that were fighting for control of issues that did not show on the surface. Actually, both the Federal Housing Administration and the Federal Public Housing Administration had little to gain, if in truth, anything. Those representing these agencies . . . Well? The invisible opponents in the fight were:

1. The property owners
2. At least three persons representing real estate companies
3. About twenty building contractors
4. The City Plan Commission

It will be necessary to go behind the scene that was taking place on stage to reveal the circumstances surrounding each of the participants. Shall we begin with Number 4, the City Plan Commission

This was a group of exceptional young men with degrees to verify their abilities to foresee and forestall, by projected planning, the problems of large cities. Under the leadership of George Emery, the Commission had successfully put together a plan which, if implemented, would virtually guarantee the City of Detroit's ability to correct past mistakes and avoid future errors. Detroit would show the other large cities how to rid themselves of slums and other undesirable aspects. This was the Commission's brain child and they were here this morning to protect it. They could not concern themselves with minor details of whose property would be involved in the plan . . . the PLAN was pre-eminent.

These were the war years. Number 3, the building contractors, were fighting for survival. Their case could be stated simply: to spare themselves bankruptcy, they must build. To build, they must have steel; to get steel, they must have the approval of the government to release the steel. They were here to fight as viciously as they had to, because it was a matter of survival.

It was late when the powerful real estate companies acknowledged that Detroit was growing in the direction of the northwest. There, smack-dab in the middle of its path, was a group of disreputable shacks owned by some black people who had the audacity to dream of building homes on these lots some day. Absolutely preposterous! It was unthinkable to entertain the thought that this would be allowed when billions of dollars were at stake. So the wheels began moving. First, all loans were denied if the property was located in this area. Therefore, no repairs, no rehabilitation, and certainly no new buildings. Next, proof in writing of the ability of these "dreamers" to develop this land. A group was hired to "poll" the property owners and to obtain answers to pertinent questions: (a) Do you wish to improve your property? (b) Have you tried to get a loan to finance your costs? (c) May we take pictures of your property? Point out the things you wish to improve.

The property owners were most cooperative. Pictures were taken and the ones that suited their purposes were used in a booklet entitled *Be It Ever So Tumbled*. The pamphlet was articulate and persuasive, closing with the question, "Shall we allow a handful of hapless dreamers to stand in the way of a potential million dollars in taxes which the city could collect annually?"

The goal of the real estate companies was to clear the land; re-subdivide it into fifty-foot-frontage lots, and extend the type of housing that was found in Palmer Woods. The cost of these homes would range from 40 to 60 thousand dollars. The brokers as well as the developers would make a substantial profit. They sought the help of the city by using the subtle sound of tax dollars as a means of persuasion. But none of this would be possible if the present owners were not stopped in their bid for F.H.A. housing in the area. The strategy: prevent any permanency in the area, insist upon the temporary units

(F.P.H.A.), talk about the debt owed to the fighting forces and their families . . . . their need for shelter . . . . Promise the landowners that enough lumber could be salvaged to build barracks for them in Inkster . . . . until some arrangements could be worked out to the satisfaction of all concerned. Promise. Talk. But GET THEM OFF THE LAND!!!

The landowners were here this morning to support their chosen representative. They had the land. They wanted to have decent homes. They had read *Be It Ever So Tumbled.* One of the residents worked in Bloomfield Hills, had seen it, and had brought it home. A private meeting had been called to discuss it.

Most of the landowners' meetings had been private. They had ways of communicating by a gesture of the hand, a tilt of the head, or the raising of an eyebrow. They knew some of the people who talked from both sides of their mouths. They knew some of the people who were sympathetic to their cause but had to be careful because of political ambitions. They knew some of the people who were to be avoided at all times. They felt that they were right, but they knew that they were powerless by themselves. They would have to merge, form a coalition with those whose goals were synonymous.

In this atmosphere of cross-currents of hopes, ideas, and goals, the gavel sounded. The crowd pressed inward from the halls and the hearing began.

In the hush that came over the crowd, the acting chairman of the Common Council stated the purpose of the meeting. A note was passed to him just as he was about to sit down. He read it. In substance, it stated that a request had been made for F.H.A. assistance in the community, but realizing the standards required by the F.H.A., the Council was inclined to favor the adoption of the project presented by the Federal Public Housing Administration. This seemed feasible, because the units were readily available, and it would allow more time to decide what should be done on a permanent basis.

"MR. CHAIRMAN!" exploded like thunder. Some wanted to be recognized to express agreement. Others (and Sally was sure the others were the property owners and the builders) wanted to demand an opportunity to discuss the subject.

This was how a meeting began that held the future development of a community as a pawn. Tempers flared. People shouted
at each other. The chairman banged his gavel time and time
again. As a last resort, the chairman said he would allow only
those people to address the body that were duly-appointed
representatives.

Sally got to her feet and wondered how visible her trembling
was to this multitude. She found her voice.

"Mr. Chairman, Ladies and Gentlemen. As spokesman for the
landowners, we want to be allowed to develop our property —
to build homes with government-insured financing. Many of
our neighbors are working side by side with homeowners who
are paying off their mortgages through F.H.A. We sympathize
with the members of the Armed Forces and their families' need
for shelter. However, ours is not the only area with space for
temporary units to house their families. We, too, as American
citizens, have a right to a comfortable shelter. Some of us have
been seeking a home for a long time. We bought this land with
this one thought in mind. Would you deny us this right?"

The meeting ended in chaos. Nothing was decided.

As Sally went back to the parking lot, she remembered the
many times that her mother had told her what Jack Williams
had said in Alabama. . . .

"If you folks don't put in a crop, GET OFF MY LAND!"
. . . . The armed guard in Virginia, "If he don't show up for
work in the mines tomorrow, you'll have to get out of the house
. . . company rules!"

And now, in Detroit, even though we own the land, we are
being told to "get off" because we are not able to develop it
the way some people think it should be developed. We had
counted on something happening at this hearing that would
be favorable to us; now, we wonder. . . .

Small knots of neighbors stood around talking quietly. There
was no sign given for a secret meeting and everybody eventually drifted on home.

Lizzie and Sally went over the things that had been said
at the City Hall and tried to fathom the meaning behind every
statement.

155

Lizzie stood for a minute and put her head to one side. "You remember when we wrote to Henry Ford to get your Dad his job?"

Sally remembered. She could recall it very clearly.

Lizzie went on, "Let's write to the President!"

Sally had learned to expect anything when Lizzie paused and put her head to the side.

"Why not?"

Sally got paper and pencil and began to draft a letter. They stated the case as briefly as they could and came directly to the point:

Dear Mr. President:

As property owners, we have requested to have assistance from the newly formed F.H.A. We would like these questions answered:

What prohibits people in this community with good credit ratings from getting loans to improve their property?

What is the difference in our community and the one just west of us, other than they are white and we are black? They are already approved for F.H.A.

May we have a representative of F.H.A. to come to Detroit to answer our questions in detail, please?

Most respectfully yours,
Lizzie Parker

It was a lot less trouble to address the President than it had been to address Mr. Ford. This letter was on its way to President Delano Roosevelt, Washington, D. C.

MR. FOLEY'S DECISION

About two weeks later, an answer came. Those who couldn't come over to read it had it read to them over the phone.

Dear Mrs. Parker:

Your letter poses a number of questions that require our attention. Since a number of letters with basically the same

156

questions have been received by this department, we are sending a representative to Detroit as you suggested.

Mr. Raymond Foley will be in Detroit on April 24th at the University of Detroit, at 7:30 o'clock. We will be pleased to have you direct your questions to him.

Thank you for your kind letter.

Yours very truly,

No one remembered who signed the letter . . . but Lizzie and a number of the neighbors were present to talk to Mr. Foley. They entered him on the "friendly" side of their ledger. He would have a chance to prove himself in a very short time. The occasion: a meeting in the office of the City Plan Commission.

The real estate interests sought to bolster their position by prevailing upon Mr. Emery to present his "Master Plan." At the unveiling of the Plan, it was noted with interest how much emphasis had been put on the need for open space in order to be able to execute the Plan. The statement was made that it was of utmost importance to leave the land unhampered by anything of a permanent nature. Chalk up another score for the opposition.

The property owners persisted in their plea for F.H.A. and were told again that this request was impossible to honor. They maintained that they had not had an opportunity to be heard. They asked permission to invite Mr. Foley. It was granted.

The place: the City Planners Office. The builders came. The representatives of F.P.H.A. were there. Mr. Raymond Foley and his staff were there. Sally and a neighbor, Mrs. Williams, were there to represent the owners of the property.

As the groups gathered, tension mounted. Each group made an obvious effort to isolate itself. When the meeting was called to order, the half-hearted attempt to be civil was soon discarded and replaced with yelling, swearing, finger-pointing, pounding, and fist-shaking. Why there were so many men representing the F.P.H.A. has never been known. They outnumbered the builders and were far more vicious. The meeting was turned into a confrontation between the two groups and boiled closer to a "free-for-all."

Mrs. Williams owned two lots. Sally and her husband owned a lot, and Sally's mother and father, the Parkers, owned a lot. There were thirteen streets in the Eight Mile Community, with little houses of varying shapes and sizes standing on the rear of many of the lots. The front of the lots was reserved for "permanent homes." Only one house in the entire community was considered a "home". This family, having exhausted all efforts to get money to build through the banks in Detroit, had gone outstate and arranged for a mortgage to construct their eight-room house. It was beautiful.

Mr. Emery had lost control of the meeting, and at any moment someone was going to strike the first blow!

Sally and Mrs. Williams were shaking with fright. Out of sheer desperation, Sally stood up. She was ignored and she began to feel foolish and embarrassed. Then she felt tears spilling out of her eyes. Someone saw her distress and shouted above the clamor, "This lady wants to say something."

In the silence that followed, Sally had trouble finding her voice. Finally, she blurted, "We just want decent homes on the land we've struggled to buy . . . and the chance to pay for them through F.H.A."

At this, the City Planner's staff and the Public Housing group turned on Sally. They wanted to know how many times they had to repeat that the community could not qualify for F.H.A. One of the men advanced, shaking his finger, "You're just afraid or ashamed to have the shadow of one of our temporary units fall on your tarpaper shacks. . . ."

"Mr. Chairman," it was Mr. Foley, trying to get the attention of Mr. Emery. The volume of noise had subsided now and Mr. Foley was given permission to speak. "Gentlemen, the question regarding the qualifications of the community has come up several times. I would like to decide for myself . . ."

He could no longer be heard. The men now directed their hostility toward Mr. Foley. Mr. Emery sent one of his staff to get maps, drafts, and other pertinent data.

"We have prepared information on every existing structure in that area. It has been evaluated and classified as a SLUM! You can't go in there!"

158

The staff member returned and began spreading out an enormous amount of material, and Mr. Emery continued, "I know the law, and the government is NOT going to guarantee money to be spent in a slum!"

He bent over the maps now and cleared his throat to explain and translate the codes.

Mr. Foley looked at the papers briefly and said calmly, "This represents your opinion. I would like to see the area and make my own evaluation."

"It took my staff six months to gather this information! And you ignore it ALL?"

"Not ignore . . . just give me an opportunity to see it for myself."

Mr. Emery made little effort to conceal his anger. "We will re-convene in three days from now, at 9:00 in the morning . . . This meeting is adjourned until then."

He banged his gavel and walked briskly from the room.

The undiminished anger was not that readily dismissed. Men plopped hats on heads, grabbed briefcases, and stalked out.

Sally and Mrs. Williams sat for a while in the empty room gathering their composure. They began talking quietly. It was clear from this meeting that the city, through the Planning Commission, was throwing its strength behind public housing. The builders were forced to become allied with the landowners and Mr. Foley for obvious reasons.

In three days, they would be sitting in this same room to hear the decision that would determine the future of their community. Plans had to be made . . . yes, every single family had to know what had happened today . . . not only what had happened, but the electrifying news that Mr. Foley himself was coming out to see for himself what the area looked like in order to make a decision! Mrs. Williams said that she would call all the people on six streets; Sally would call the families on the other seven streets. The message reminded one of Paul Revere . . . "CLEAN UP! FIX UP! MR. FOLEY IS COMING!!!"

That night, bonfires were visible throughout the neighborhood. Curtains were snatched down and washed, windows were washed, curtains were ironed and re-hung, yards were raked, lawns were mowed, shrubbery was trimmed; and every possible thing was done to increase their chances of qualifying for Federal Housing Administration assistance.

The next morning, Sally's phone rang about 10:00. "There are two expensive cars with some very distinguished-looking men driving slowly down our street . . . Do you suppose???"

The message went from street to street; phones were answered quietly, "Yes, they've just turned down this street." . . . "No, they are going very slowly, watching everything — keep on praying!"

A cogent Mr. Emery called the meeting to order. All of the concerned parties were present to a man, and Mrs. Williams and Sally could have been on the Isle of Capri as far as their presence being acknowledged. The men walked into the room, grim-faced and silent.

"The first and perhaps the only thing on the agenda is the report from Mr. Raymond Foley." Mr. Emery then sat down with an expression of strained tolerance.

Mr. Foley addressed the chair, "Gentlemen, I'm sorry, Ladies and Gentlemen. I visited the area and my staff and I found . . . Well, to come right to the point, the builders can start tomorrow, if they are ready."

There was a split second of silence, and then men sprang from their chairs with such frenzy and with such a torrent of vindictive expletives that Mr. Foley seemed in danger of physical injury. The building contractors, jubilant in their victory and suddenly aware of the situation, stood firmly by Mr. Foley.

The gathering had exploded. There was no possible way to handle the decision without creating an outlet for the lava to escape. It came in the form of a compromise. The F.P.H.A. would be allowed to use 300 parcels for the temporary units. The contractors were given 300 houses to build, and they worked out a pro-rated amount for each company. The wonderful magical plan of the Commission would have to be implemented on another site.

Mrs. Williams and Sally went home with the joyful news. No one felt that it was less than a glorious victory for the property owners. By the help of God, they would have a permanent toe-hold in the community, and with His guidance, they would develop it in spite of opposition.

Temporary units: quonset huts and prefabricated structures of varying sizes and shapes magically appeared overnight. Simultaneously, thirteen developing companies, each choosing a street, dug basements and built three hundred permanent F.H.A. approved homes. Lizzie and Sally joined the neighbors in "Thanks to God" for them. Bob, Sally's husband, bought the house next door to the family house and moved his wife and daughter in — to have the never-before-enjoyed experience of living in a brand new house. (See p. 189 for map of the 8 Mile Road Community).

A GENIUS IN THE FAMILY

Friday, December 5, 1941 . . . Parent Teacher Conference at Higginbotham. Sally was turning her wide wedding band 'round and 'round as she sat listening to Enid's teacher.

"Mrs. Hayward, Enid is a darling child, but she doesn't follow directions. She does beautiful work, but only if she wants to. I really don't think she tries . . . she daydreams."

"Do you have any suggestions? I would gladly try them. You see, I've tried all the things I know. I have spanked her when she brought notes home; I have made her stay in from play; I have offered her rewards for good marks on her card . . . they just don't work," said Sally.

It was like they were reading a play — the same lines time after time, teacher after teacher. Sally wondered how long it would go on. The drama continued when Sally reached home — talking to Enid, promising, threatening, trying to direct her toward goals that Sally thought she should attain.

A giant hand turned a page in history, and suddenly the papers were full of PEARL HARBOR!!! Over 4,000 Americans were killed, wounded, or missing as a result of Japan's attack. War was declared against Japan on December 8, 1941. A few

161

days later, the United States declared war against Germany and Italy; the country was fighting on two fronts. This war was different. President Roosevelt had declared it, and he was the sort of man who included Negroes in his thinking. Furthermore, it was unnerving the way the Japanese had been right here in America, bowing and talking so politely at the very moment they were attacking Pearl Harbor. Dealing with that kind of deceit has a tendency to draw people together. "It is high time to strike a blow at Italy in retaliation for invading Ethiopia," summed up the way many in the Eight Mile community felt.

Time passes swiftly when dynamic decisions are not hanging like suspended swords. The community was resting on its oars and handling minor problems rather well when it became aware of plans to develop the land south of Pembroke from Greenlawn to Wyoming. A small notice was placed in the legal calendar of the paper:

> Petition #--- begs to have the code changed from one family to multiple and light industry, site located - Pembroke Wyoming area. Hearing Thursday at ten A.M.

The regulars got back into uniform and presented themselves for duty to guard the gains the neighborhood had made. They expressed their disapproval. The petition was denied.

The next attempt sought only multiple dwelling usage without the light industry. The community had a harder fight on its hands this time. Mr. Abrams was determined to put eighty families directly across the street on Pembroke's south side in a four-block area. He requested and got a hearing before the Common Council.

"And they have repeatedly rejected my efforts to build these beautiful units to provide shelter for their own people," said Mr. Abrams, pointing to an artist's sketch of his plans.

Councilwoman Mary Beck was impressed with his presentation. "It looks like a very nice project to me, and I think he should be allowed to go ahead." Then, turning to Sally, who was the spokesman for the community, she continued, "This is his property and he has the right to develop it."

162

"We do not deny that he has rights, but so do we, and his rights END where ours begin," Sally said quietly, and then she enumerated incidents of differing attitudes of renters and buyers. The apartment units were not allowed, and once more the best interests of a young neighborhood had been served.

"DON'T CHANGE HORSES IN MID-STREAM." So, in 1944, the Parkers and the Haywards went to the polls and helped to elect Franklin D. Roosevelt for an historic fourth term.

Enid had celebrated her tenth birthday in September and had shown little or no improvement in her work at school. Sally continued to worry about her child. Often she tried to figure out the reasons for Enid's behavior, and her mind circled around and around, examining everything that could remotely contribute to her lack of interest in school. She never failed to include the possibility of the spinal injection having had unknown side effects. As a last resort, Sally asked the school psychologist to test Enid to determine what kind of special help she needed.

"Have her ready at 8:30 and report to Dr. ——— in Room 506. She will be here all day with the testing. Plan to pick her up about 4:00 or 4:15," the assistant said.

"Thank you. Will she know that you are testing her to see how retarded she is?"

"She'll know that she is being tested. She may not know what we're looking for."

It took a few weeks to evaluate the test and compile the results. Meanwhile, Enid was playing "hooky" and spending the days with her friends. Sally would eventually find out about it and present herself at the friend's house to have a talk with the parents. Too often, it was only one parent, and Sally was told in one version or another, "Ah, Miz Hayward, you too hard on her. Kids got to have some fun. You cain't raise her in a band box. These kids now-a-days is different than when you and me came along."

Sally got the letter telling her to come down to discuss the results of the test.

"Well, Mrs. Hayward, now that we have the results of the test, I think we can begin to see the reason for Enid's behavior. You have a very exceptional youngster. She scored 178 on the IQ test. It's no wonder she is bored with public school. We recommend that you try to get her in one of the schools for exceptional children. Failing that, or while you are making the necessary arrangements, get her out of public school before she reacts to school by developing a "phobia."

Sally sat with her mouth hanging open, trying to absorb what she had been told.

"Does she complain about headaches or illness?" asked the psychologist.

"Yes, but I think she's just trying to give me an excuse for not going to school."

"It is not unusual for children like your daughter to have the sensation of actual pain in a structured situation. I think if I were you, I would take her out of school until I could find the right learning atmosphere for her." He rose to leave.

"Thank you, doctor . . . ." Sally was in a daze.

Poor ignorant parents, thought Sally. We bring the kids up the best we can and then get an order to find $1,000 to pay for a semester of private schooling . . . poor people like herself and Bob . . . take the kid out of school? What would she do all day long? Just more time to run around with a gang of no-good youngsters who never wanted to go to school in the first place . . . Sally wondered further how to handle the news, and deep down, if it were REALLY authentic.

"That's what the doctor said," Sally reported to the family that night.

"Well," said Bob, "I'm at my wit's end."

"I can't see letting a kid that age out to pasture," John said.

"What do you think we ought to do?" Sally wanted to know.

"You asked the people for advice — they gave it to you. I'd follow it," Lizzie said. "Now I know we can't put her in a private school, but we can stop forcing her to go to Mumford — maybe she can take up drawing or something."

One thing they all agreed on. It was not going to be an easy time to live through.

JOHN PASSES

The next five years saw Enid go from the "motorcycle gang" to having a band of her own, while taking a correspondence course in drawing, giving everything her characteristic cursory interest except the persistent young man in uniform.

Sally looked at the nineteen-year-old war veteran and tried to explain to him, "You have no idea of the responsibility of a marriage . . . being the head of a family. . . ."

"Mrs. Hayward, if I was mature enough to go overseas and face bullets, I think I'm mature enough to marry your daughter."

"Let me talk it over with her Daddy when he comes in. I'll let you know."

Bob's first answer was a flat "NO."

"Well, I don't know, Hon, you're here with her all the time, and I know you haven't been able to control her all the time. Maybe . . . maybe . . . Oh, my God, I don't know . . . Do what you think is best."

Sally signed, giving her daughter permission to marry, not wanting to predict disaster, yet knowing, somehow, that it was inevitable.

Sally was working; Bob made a joke of it.

"When she comes home with her pay, I have to take it and buy liniment, pills, ointments, and hire a nurse for her so she will be able to go back to work. If she's lucky, we may be able to save a dollar out of her wages."

Bob joked about the things that bothered him most. One of the things he joked about was the conditions he ran into on the road — from city to city and from state to state. One of his classics supposedly took place in Meridian, Mississippi.

"One of the men who lived their told us: 'Fell'as, there's a wonderful show down at the Bijou.' So since we had to lay over, we went. He reminded us that we had to sit in the balcony. We were a little late and had to climb a tree and get in through the back window after we had bought our tickets. It was a good show and it was funny. A guy told a joke and I laughed. Right in the middle of my laugh, one of the ushers ran up and put his hand over my mouth, 'Man, don't do that! Wait 'til the white folks get through laughing. When they tap the bell, THEN you can laugh.' Meridian is the only place I know that has 'laughing barrels' on the street, so if a Negro gets tickled, he can stick his head down in the barrel and laugh, in case some white person may be laughing somewhere in town."

Sally was on the job on April 12, 1945. She was washing the upstairs bathroom floor when the lady she was working for ran upstairs and told Sally in a trembling voice, "The President is dead!" Sally couldn't answer, and the two women cried together. The man who cared was gone!

John had shown signs of withdrawal. There would be times when he would sit for hours just looking out into space. At other times, he was too talkative, and it was hard to close a conversation. He was too weak to push his junk cart and had very little to do with his time. Reading, his favorite hobby, had to be discontinued because of failing eyesight.

Mr. Wilson knocked on the door and asked Lizzie, "Did Mr. Parker come back yet?"

"I didn't know he had gone anywhere," Lizzie said as she rushed outside. "Snyder, have you seen my husband?"

"No, I just came out on the porch a few minutes ago."

"The reason I asked," Mr. Wilson said, "he told me he was going to Clayton and wanted to get there before dark. It dawned on me awhile ago that Clayton is in Alabama."

The word spread like wildfire. "Mr. Parker is missing!" People organized search parties to comb the neighborhood. Some of the older people came over to wait by the phone in case any information was phoned in. Some also waited at Sally's house. She and all the family were out searching. The searchers broadened their circle. Still no trace of John. About 11:00 the phone rang. The police who were out with the searchers had received word that he had been found on Grand Boulevard near Woodward and had been brought to the Bethune Station. The word was relayed and the neighbors formed a caravan to escort John back home.

The desk sergeant and the whole night crew smiled and joked with the crowd as they told how John had been found standing in the middle of the Boulevard directing traffic. Every-

166

body was relieved, but none as much as Lizzie and Sally. John sat shaking hands with his friends and smiling. Bob and Sally helped him out to a car and the crowd waved goodbye to the policemen, still smiling.

All the neighbors now were concerned about John and promised to keep an eye out for him.

"The fall that caused this egg-shaped lump on his head might have brought pressure on certain nerves, resulting in his erratic behavior," the doctor said. "He is also suffering from hardening of the arteries, and when people get older . . . well . . ."

Lizzie bought a lamp that John had admired. It was far too expensive and she couldn't afford it, but "watching him enjoy the lamp is worth every penny," Lizzie would say. Maybe it symbolized the kind of home he had dreamed of.

John wandered away again, and the doctor advised putting him in a hospital. Sally was reluctant, but did not want to disobey the doctor's suggestion. She was not able to provide the kind of care her father needed 24 hours a day and she had to admit it.

After John had been in the hospital for ten days, the call came. He had slept on and could not be awakened to the turmoils of the world.

Sally put up a blockade and refused to accept it. Lizzie was strong. She had become much more deeply involved with the church.

"We had him a long time and I'm sure he was tired." Sally did not respond, but lifted her head and studied the cloud formations.

"Death has spared us for a long time. Not since 1925 when your Aunt Ada passed — and before then . . ." Sally would not be drawn into the conversation. Sometimes she acted as if she was not sure where she was. Her mind did not function. She was numb.

Lizzie led the procession, a nurse at her side, followed by Sally, leaning heavily on the arm of Bob. Behind them, Enid and other relatives and close friends formed a solemn line.

The soloist began, "Going home, going home . . . . ." Sally

screamed. The inside of her chest had expanded to unbearable dimensions.

"Papa wanted a home . . . On Jordan's stormy banks — And cast a wishful eye . . . ." Sally could hear her father singing or humming . . . "I am bound for the promised land . . ."

The service ended and John was laid to rest.

The impossible task was somehow accomplished. The pieces were picked up and life did go on.

Lizzie was alone now, and Bob and Sally were never quite relaxed, especially at night.

"Mama, are you all right? I thought I heard a noise, Bob and I came over to see what it was."

"I'm all right, but I heard something too. I guess it was across the alley or somewhere."

The intense listening and the jumping out of bed, sometimes twice in one night, caused Lizzie to think seriously of selling her home and going to live with Bob and Sally. Of course this meant selling her furniture, too, or finding a larger house. Musing over the thought of living somewhere other than the Eight Mile community was something new.

Lizzie had a feeling of attainment when she looked at the neighborhood. She had been here at the beginning and had been a part of the moving force that had brought all this into being. Bringing it to this point had been accomplished by going as far as the State Supreme Court to win an appeal that had said in substance: Detroit cannot condemn private homes to provide recreational facilities unless it first considers its own land less than three blocks away. Using its land for a tree nursery is not sufficient cause to delete it from consideration.

It was during this long legal battle about recreation that there had been evidence of less than a solid front. The attitudes and goals of residents living in different situations had shown in a wide variance.

By some strange coincidence, former Shacktown had still been solidly black, while the neighborhoods on three sides had been solidly white. The fourth side was the county line and city limits.

Mr. Slatkin, a new developer, had emphasiezd this racial difference by building a ten-foot solid wood fence running parallel to Pembroke, in order to assure privacy on his property, which was bounded by Outer Drive on the south, Wyoming on the west, Pembroke on the north, and Cherrylawn on the east. (See p. 191).

The residents of the Eight Mile community had been proud of the neat brick homes and those brightly-painted frame houses. They had felt that it was an insult to have a wall built to separate them in this manner. A member of the secret committee had described the following incident at a meeting held by the community:

"After several calls, I was successful in getting Mr. Slatkin to the phone. I asked, 'Mr. Slatkin, may we have an appointment with you?'

" 'For what reason?' he inquired.

" 'We would like to discuss the impact on the community as a whole of your having built the solid fence, south of Pembroke. We consider it an affront.'

" 'It's of little consequence to me what you consider it to be,' he answered.

" 'In our opinion, it is not in the best interests of community relations,' I persisted.

" 'East is east and west is west and never the twain shall meet . . . at least not in our day. I see no reason or purpose in meeting with your committee.' And that is how the conversation ended."

The wall remains around Mr. Slatkin's apartment complex, but in the late 1950s, black families began building and occupying $30- and $40,000 homes on Cherrylawn south of Pembroke. Also adjacent to the Slatkin wall stands the $400,000 Oak Grove A.M.E. Church.

Lizzie now looked at all the homes that sheer grit and prayer had brought into existence, and yet, there was an unsatisfied longing deep inside. In quiet moments, when her mind ran free, she recalled a promise. Her home was 19928 Wisconsin, but it was not her dream.

"Maybe it wasn't to be fulfilled. We have come a long way, crossing five states, Michigan making the sixth. Surely, in all those miles and years, if it were going to come true, it would have by now," she thought wistfully.

LEAVING THE EIGHT MILE COMMUNITY

Working together for the common good has its own reward, but the neighbors who had come through so many hardships only because they had been able to lean on each other wanted to show their gratitude in a special way to one of their members. A group volunteered to serve as a scholarship committee to accept gifts and donations from friends and other interested persons. These they paid out to the Detroit Institute of Technology for Sally's tuition.

Here she would take a pre-law course for two years; then she would go on to the Detroit College of Law. When Sally was told of the generous offer, she was without words to express how grateful she was. Her mother would get her wish after all. Her daughter was going to college. Sally was a grown woman, but the old fear still haunted her when faced with a challenge that took her to uncharted surroundings.

Yes, she was grateful, but she still had to jut out her chin and brace herself to wade into it. Since her daughter had insisted on marrying at age seventeen, Sally would be the college student in the family. By now Enid had two children: a little girl, Richarde, and a baby boy, Scottie.

Sally came over one evening after supper and found her mother sitting quietly in John's favorite chair.

"Mama, what would you think if I told you that I've been looking for another house?"

"Another house?" asked Lizzie, sitting forward, "Where?"

"Everywhere. Just looking and asking around."

"Well?"

170

"Since you agreed to live with us, I didn't know how you would feel about leaving the neighborhood if we found something somewhere else."

"We? What does Bob think about leaving the neighborhood?"

"He doesn't mind, if we find something we really like." They sat for a little while, saying nothing. Sally knew that her mother's mind was shifting gear and that she had better complete the picture.

"We're going to need four bedrooms, one for your granddaughter. She and that husband of hers are not going to make it, and she's hinting about coming back home and bringing the kids."

"Yes, at least four bedrooms. That's a lot of house you're talking about." The upsurge in Lizzie's spirit could be detected in her voice.

"You all made up your minds to sell?"

"Yep! We want to do it quietly — no signs, but we think we can find a buyer."

"I see. You must'a been thinking this for some time. What brought it to a head?" asked Lizzie. Sally looked out of the window and blew her breath out through puffed cheeks.

"The neighborhood is not like it used to be. It's been split ever since we got two kinds of housing in here. When you have to fight inside and outside at the same time, progress is hard to come by."

"The fact that we wasn't together broke wide open during the last fight," Lizzie recalled. "The nerve — two different committees, both supposing to represent the community."

"I'm tired of getting the back-lash from people who have no knowledge of the history of this community. I don't want to walk away and leave the 'old guard,' but I'm tired. They won't listen when I ask them to get somebody else as spokesman." Lizzie remembered how she had encouraged Sally to accept this job, and Sally recalled minutes like the one when she had stood up, knees buckling, in the City Planners Office and had given the message of the community to Mr. Foley in the midst of derision . . . how she had sat, stomach tied in knots, in the Council Chamber and had talked quietly to Mary Beck

171

about holding on to the one-family code for the neighborhood. And how she had sat listening to Ramon Martinez arguing the condemnation case in the State Supreme Court. God had given them the victory in every instance, but she was tired.

Coming out of her reverie, Sally continued, "And the other thing is, Enid needs a different atmosphere if she's to make a career for herself. I think she has a chance, if she doesn't get caught in the 'undertow' — that's the part you got to watch, since her marriage didn't work."

"I understand what you mean. We'll have to help her with the kids and give her a chance," Lizzie said thoughtfully. And it all began to fall into place — the continued search for the home she dreamed about one night in Alabama, over 40 years ago.

The bent hammered-down nails, the closets minus doors, the corners that were not quite straight, and the general unsoundness of the structure made Lizzie less and less willing to accept this as home without at least one more try.

Sally and Bob had thought that their house was beautiful at first. Everything had seemed exciting when they had moved in: the little concrete stoop too small for a porch, the living room with the large picture window, the dining niche, the tiny compact kitchen, the two bedrooms and bath on the first floor, and the large finished space on the second floor.

Lately, though, the niche had seemed too small to be useful and the kitchen too tiny, and Sally had grown weary of putting everything in the hall to allow her to get around the bed each time she cleaned the bedrooms.

Bob was keenly aware of the way some of the newcomers felt about his wife. He was a railroad man and had to be away from home a lot. Many of the residents did not know who he was — that is, the fact that he was Sally's husband, Enid's father, or Mrs. Parker's son-in-law. He had heard a few unguarded remarks that he had felt were uncalled-for and unjustifiable.

Bob recalled the incident a few years back when he had become aware of a conversation going on behind him while riding the bus. "Old lady Parker and her whole family makes me sick. They think they're so much, always up in the white folks' face trying to tell them what to do."

"Ain't it the truth. I was glad when Enid was kept off the Easter program. She tries to talk so proper."

"I know what you mean. It did me good to see her standing there and the Sunday School teacher passed ice cream to everybody around her. When Enid finally asked for some, the teacher told her that the ice cream was just for the children who were on the program."

"Good enough for her."

Bob had wanted to look back to see who was talking, but he had kept on pretending to read his paper instead.

"East side, west side, all around the town" . . . looking at houses. Sally would report to the family her findings.

"I saw two very nice houses today — only three bedrooms though —"

"All of them have only two or three bedrooms," Lizzie said. "I can sleep in the den or the recreation room; I'm not that . . ."

"NO! Everybody's going to have their own private bedroom. We've got time. I'll just keep on looking," Sally said.

The organization that tried to represent the total community kept on trying to do the things that made living conditions better. It asked for "Stop" signs at dangerous corners, for mail boxes, for loitering to be discontinued on Eight Mile and for an end to the loud music from the record shop. One market owner refused to hire any help from the neighborhood. The organization asked for a boycott. He was forced out of business.

"If you want to sell something, make it attractive," Bob said as he climbed up the ladder to continue painting the house a gleaming white. Sally, meantime, was busy going back and forth to the basement carrying the dining room chairs and varnishing them. "Four down and two to go," she said to herself. Bob had told her to wait and let him take care of the chairs, but she would surprise him and have them all done — an awkward step, and Sally and the chair went tumbling to the basement floor! For a fraction of an instant she lay there, and then she tried to get up. Her right foot dangled oddly. "Bob!!!" she screamed, engulfed in fear and pain. "BOB!!" She

173

saw herself trying to walk for the rest of her life with only one foot.

Bob raced down the steps and started to try to lift his wife while asking, "What were you doing? What were you trying to do with these chairs?" He was angry, but he was more afraid. "Where are you hurt?"

"My foot. NO, don't try to move me, it's broken!" Sally began to cry. Bob stood hesitant for a second. "I'll call the hospital . . ."

"No," said Sally, "Call a doctor and he will call a hospital."

"I can't leave you just laying there on the floor . . ."

"I'll be all right. It's not so painful. The doctor will know what to do, but I'd better just stay here until he comes."

Bob rushed upstairs and tried to dial the number to call the doctor, but he found that it was like stringing beads with mittens on. The neighbor across the street came over, called for him, and helped to calm him down.

The doctor came and bound the injured foot to a piece of wood. Then he called for an ambulance to take Sally to the hospital. She had broken her ankle and had taken a chip off her heel bone. That ended her house hunting, but the ad in the paper had already caught the attention of a buyer and he was anxious to close the deal.

Bob and Lizzie spent their time visiting Sally and searching for a four-bedroom house when they were not on the job. The bone specialist concluded that an operation to clean out all foreign matter and to place a steel rod to serve as an ankle would be best for Sally. After a three-week stay in the hospital, Sally was allowed to come home.

The first order of business was to sign the papers that gave ownership of their home to the new buyer. The check was deposited in the bank. Ninety days after that date, they were expected to vacate.

"I think we've found it," Bob announced when he returned one evening. And he exhibited a broad smile that spoke eloquently. Sally's questions poured out, "Does it have four bedrooms? Where is it? What color is it? How much is it?"

"I'll let your mother tell you about it," he said, as Lizzie rushed in, looking pleased.

"I think we've found it," she said, the identical words that Bob had said. "It's brick and has a fireplace, plenty of bedrooms, a big dining room . . . it even has glass doorknobs. I know you'll like it."

"I wish I could see it."

"I'm going to see about getting some crutches for you as soon as the doctor says you can handle them," Bob said. "You'll see it."

He was not easily excited, but there was something about this house that made him almost as eager as Lizzie was to investigate the possibilities of buying it.

TIME, — they wanted it to leap forward for Sally to get better, and to go as slowly as possible in terms of the 90 days and the arrangements to get the house. The elderly couple who was selling the house was in no hurry. They had all the time in the world. In order to do the things they had planned, they asked almost a third of the purchase price as down payment, and that required TIME!

Lizzie mortgaged her home for the amount needed, in addition to Bob's check in order to close the deal. The 90 days expired, and the sum of $100 per month was paid as rent to the buyer of Bob's house.

When the attorney said that he had found out that the property they were buying had once belonged to Henry and Clara Ford, Lizzie gave Sally a knowing look, as if to say, "We've finally come home."

It had all been done quietly and took the neighbors by surprise, many of whom were sorry to see the Parkers leave. "Moving to a twelve room house, huh? That's the Parkers for ya'," summed up the feelings of others. But all who knew Lizzie had to admit that "stamina" is made of stern stuff and lacks an abundance of sensitivity. Lizzie Parker had stamina. It was characteristic of her to pursue her dream.

THE KEY TO THE CITY

Their membership remained at Oak Grove and the family continued to serve with that congregation. Sally had used the past few years to broaden her education, switching from the study of law to teacher training. Lizzie had become well-known as an evangelist in many parts of the country. But Enid traveled the most, going to foreign countries to fill engagements as a singing artist.

"You mean to tell me, this is the KEY TO THE CITY OF DETROIT?" Lizzie held the box containing the long golden key. She fondled it lovingly.

"We entertainers have a name for it, Grandma." Enid laughed heartily. Then, realizing that her grandmother would hardly appreciate the joke, she sobered and went on to tell about the plans.

"The Mayor has declared October 22, 1961, to be 'ENID THORTON DAY.' The pictures of the key presentation should be in the paper today or tomorrow. And I'm supposed to do something promotional with the Pistons . . . that's a new basketball team. They will be known like the Detroit Tigers."

Sally took off her white gloves, still feeling the glow of having her picture taken in the Mayor's office with her daughter Enid receiving the "key" to the City! Enid may not have thought much of it, but to Lizzie and Sally, it was a significant milestone . . . the granddaughter of Lizzie being given the "KEY" TO THE CITY OF DETROIT!!!!

October 22 was the date of Enid's concert at the Ford Auditorium. There were two other concerts that same evening, one at Cobo Hall and the other at the Masonic Temple. Enid was the lesser known of the three artists, but the review she got was high in its praise of her talent.

Oblivious to everything except the activity of her first graders, who were classifying food and finding out how it grows as well as learning new words, Sally was not aware of her principal standing just outside the door. Mrs. Taylor knocked softly and beckoned to Sally.

"Go on with your work, children, I'll be right back," and Sally stepped into the hall.

"Mrs. Hayward, President Kennedy has been shot!"

"Oh, no, no, my God, no," Sally was whispering, fearing to say anything aloud; sound might add credibility . . . Mrs. Taylor's face was drawn. "I'll keep you informed." She moved quickly down the hall to the next room. Sally stood — as inert as the clay animals which the children were making. "I've got to go back in there — they'll know something is wrong. How do you tell children about a tragedy?" She walked as briskly as she could to a window and stood looking out. With her back still toward the class, she said, "Boys and girls, you may begin putting things away now; take time to clean up quietly — I'll look at your work tomorrow."

They knew. They didn't know what it was, but the way they tiptoed around, whispering and getting things into cupboards, then sitting with hands folded, you could tell that they knew something was wrong.

"It's almost time for us to go home. President Kennedy has been in an accident. When you get home, mother will tell you more about it."

"How? . . . Is he hurt bad? . . . He's dead, isn't he?"

"Let's just put our heads down and rest. We will get our wraps in a few minutes. I don't know the answers to your questions, children. We will find out when we get home."

There were others wiping their eyes in their cars on the way home. Sally remembered the last time she had cried over the death of a President; she had received the news on her knees while scrubbing the floor.

Lizzie was at the television when Sally came in. The news bulletin kept repeating all the details that had been released at that time. The children burst through the door and ran to Sally, threw their arms around her, and having held back as long as they could, hid their faces and sobbed. Scottie and Richarde had run all the way from Doty School. Now they were home and joining a nation, weeping for a man they had learned to love.

THE NEW "LEADERS"

In 1964, Reverend Martin Luther King, Jr., was guest speaker for the General Conference of the A.M.E. Church, held in Cincinnati, Ohio. His speech was recorded — and Lizzie bought one of the albums. She never grew tired of listening to him. She got an emotional impact every time she heard the speech. Ideas and philosophies are sometimes difficult to pinpoint. One hears heated discussions and wonders how deeply-rooted some of the dogma is which is being expounded. The non-violent preaching of Martin Luther Knig, Jr., took deep roots and spread. Lizzie and her family were among the thousands who felt that he was a God-sent man for troubled times.

Disquieting things began to surface at about this time, things that Lizzie tried to reason out. Many family discussions centered around these unusual concepts. On the rare occasions when Enid was at home, the family sought her evaluation.

"What do you hear out there? What does it mean? Who are the people behind this trend? How big is their following? Does it make sense to you?"

Enid wasn't sure about some of the questions or many of the answers, but she had heard enough to realize that a great many young intelligent folks had discarded the description "Negro" and had embraced the once-fighting word "black." Some were still allowing themselves to be thrown in jail, following the non-violent movement, while others were saying, "NO WAY! DEMAND JOBS! DEMAND LAND! . . . They owe it to us for the years of free slave labor we gave them to build this country!" Along with these demands was untarnished HATE!

"Are people listening to these young leaders?" Lizzie asked.

"Yes," said Enid. "Some of the groups go under the name of 'Negro History Classes,' and they give a lot of information about the ex-slaves and what they have contributed to this country."

"Nothing wrong with that. We made the board take a book out of the schools that had the word 'nigger' in it and replace it with a history book about Negroes."

"Don't say 'nee-grows,' Grandma," said Enid, a little edgy. "Say 'black people.'"

Lizzie wanted to think seriously about what was being said by many of the young people, but she didn't know how to get around the enormous wall of hate they were building.

"Hate is like a powerful acid — it destroys the vessel that holds it, sometimes before it can harm anything else," Lizzie reasoned.

Scottie brought a notice to his great grandmother. He had found it sticking under the screen.

"Read it for me, honey," Lizzie said, handing it to Richarde. She read the notice about an important meeting that would inform the black community of important issues. Lizzie would attend this meeting and find out for herself some of the answers she had been seeking from other people.

The young speaker was informed, intelligent, and fiery. A donation of $2.00 entitled one to a booklet that showed pictures of police brutality, dogs biting people, bodies hanging lifeless from trees, and the stories that went with the pictures. Anyone having suffered an injustice at any time would empathize with the speaker. He closed by making at least four demands, then asked if there were questions.

Lizzie raised her hand, the speaker nodded in her direction. "Yes?"

"If you succeeded in getting the states you ask for, do you have a plan to create jobs for the people? How would you get the money to support the gover'ment you plan to set up?"

"Don't you worry about it, Auntie. If you want to help, you can do it by taking care of our young children and leaving the business to those of us who are trained to take care of business." His answer was followed by laughter and applause. Another young man got up from the audience and said, "We don't mean no harm, but really, this organization is for people who is young like ourselves. Anybody over 30 is too old to change."

On the way home, Lizzie said to Sally, "I thought maybe we could exchange ideas . . . experience that comes from age, and young ideas . . . ."

But it had been made clear there was no common ground in their program for any exchange, and the feeling fermented while older people watched and wondered.

179

RIOT!!

"We haven't had our friends down here since we moved and sort of got things straightened out," Lizzie said. Sally and Bob agreed.

Bob got the calendar. "Let me see when I'll be in town. I'll be in on the second, the sixth and the tenth . . . Let's plan for the tenth, that's on a Sunday."

"Let's have a Fourth of July picnic in the backyard for us kids," Richarde said, jumping up and down.

"Yea!" yelled Scottie, "A picnic, and we can ask our friends. Can we, Granddad? Can we?"

Their mother had brought swings, a slide, and see-saw for them and they wanted to show them off to their friends.

"Well, all right, but I hope you won't run me crazy," said Sally and mumbled to herself, "I wish I could get out of doing it, but their mother's not here and somebody's got to suffer along with it, I guess."

The Fourth came. The children's friends came, broke the slide, and tore the swings down; that was the end of that.

"Remember how you were attracted to the beautiful backyard when you came down on your crutches? Well, little feet and green lawns don't mix too well — one or the other's got to go," Bob reminded Sally. "There's a park right across the street; they won't suffer from lack of exercise."

"We better start now and make a list, so we won't forget the main people," Lizzie said, and sat down, relishing the idea of getting together with old friends.

Sally was doing the writing and Bob would call out a name once in awhile. "Oh, yes — I'm glad you remembered him," as she wrote it down. It took quite a time getting addresses and phone numbers. When they knew anything, the list had grown to over twenty people.

"Oh, Lord, how will we ever manage that many folks?" Sally counted the names again.

"You're not thinking about serving dinner at the table, are you?", asked Bob.

180

"That's what I started out thinking about," answered Sally, "What did you have in mind, Mama?"

"Well, to tell you the truth, I hadn't given it a thought — Good Gracious! Twenty people?"

Lizzie walked into the dining room. It was a nice room with wood paneling and such a pretty chandelier. But you couldn't get more than twelve people to sit down in the space the extended table afforded.

"Tell you what — oh, wait a minute." Bob had miscounted. "I go OUT on the tenth!" He thought for a minute. "It might work anyway if I can get a ride to the station. What I started to say — I could barbecue some ribs and maybe two or three fryers and serve it buffet style — let the people help themselves. All you would have to worry about is plenty of salad and something cold to drink, and maybe dessert."

"That's it! That'll do it. I don't know what I'd do without you," Sally told Bob.

"You're just lucky that I said 'Yes' when you asked me," and ducked automatically, because Sally usually threw something at him whenever he made that remark.

Bob picked up the calendar again. "Wonder how I made that mistake . . . ."

"That's not the one you had at first, it's upstairs."

"What differ----?"

"It's last year's calendar. I saved it to use the pictures for a bulletin board. This is 1967."

"You don't say?" Sally outran him and locked herself in the powder room.

The phone rang incessantly. "We'll be there, I forgot what time," or, "What's the best way to get their from here?" or, "My uncle is here from down home, is it all right to bring him?" Some wanted to know if they shouldn't bring something "potluck."

Bob allowed himself plenty of time and gradually filled the large roaster with barbecued ribs. Lizzie thought she should fry the chickens. Sally gathered greens for the salad and baked a pound cake. Those who wanted it could have ice cream and cake.

A few friends had come down to help with the moving and had admired the house then, but now with things settled . . . with Sally's furniture, Lizzie's furniture, and two new chairs and lamps . . . the house looked even nicer.

The Snyders were the first to arrive. Immediately, they began to recall the things they used to make out with or do without entirely. Neighbor after neighbor joined the group and the subject never changed. The house hummed with the pleasant sound of people enjoying themselves and feeling completely relaxed. They moved a mite slower now and every head had at least a few gray strands, but their laughter was as hearty as it had been 40 years ago.

Too soon Bob had to beg off and prepare to go to work. The friend he had asked to take him to the station called. He was having trouble with his car.

"I'll take you," Sally told him, "I won't be missed. I'll be back in half an hour."

The children were busy taking groups up to the third floor and down to the basement. Other wandered out to the screened-in porch and on to the freshly-cut lawn in the back yard. Richarde served dessert to the few who had room for it.

Lizzie, white-haired and queenly, sat and talked with Mrs. Wilson. They were both widows. Mr. Wilson had died a few months after John had passed. The two women never quite finished their conversations. Lizzie was telling how she and Sally had put their "change" together and had bought this house. As she talked, it was evident that at long last, Lizzie had found the home she had been seeking since that night in Alabama so many years and tears ago.

Lizzie and Laura sat near the window that faced out on the quiet street of well-kept lawns and shade trees.

"I remember a long time ago," Lizzie began, "Mother would call me to help milk the cows about this time of evening. The sun would be going down and she would stop and look out at the beautiful colors and say, 'Lord, I wonder where my boys are tonight.' It always makes me sad when I see the sunset."

"I understand. It makes me sad too. Seems like only yesterday. I came from work . . . about this time of day, and found my husband. The nurse was still trying to work on him. He had suffered so long and you know that . . . but you're never ready for it."

Lizzie's thoughts went spinning back to all the loved ones she had lost. As she talked about John she said, " I hope you don't think I'm silly, but I often find myself hoping that John knows how happy we are in this house. He really tried . . . he would've liked this place."

"Our place is nowhere near as big as this house, but it's nice and I enjoy it. We know how much we had to go through to get where we are today, but I can't understand our young folks, can you? I mean all this talk about making the government give them five states, and making them do this and making them do that."

"They are tired, I know, and they don't want to wait as long as we waited . . . but I don't understand how they are going about the situation. I went to one of their meetings, and they politely asked me out. No, I don't understand them."

Laura sat forward in her chair. "Now, you take my oldest boy . . . ." She was interrupted in her confidential statement by Mr. Snyder.

"We were the first to get here and we don't want to wear out our welcome. I don't know when I have had such a good time. I told Bob he's going to have to come out and barbecue for me before the summer's over. I know I ate too much."

Others were drifting out through the living room to say "Goodbye".

Lizzie went out on the front porch with the guests, accepting their thanks and compliments for the wonderful time they had spent in her lovely home. The women gave her a hug and the men a handshake, enjoying the mutual friendship that had been cemented by sharing hardship together.

The last guests waved from their car as they turned the corner just as Sally drove up and braked so fast that Lizzie knew something was wrong. She ran up on the porch wide-eyed and trembling a little.

"That trip back was something else — they're going crazy over on Twelfth street! I was driving along . . . . ."

An ambulance screamed urgently and faded in the distance. Smoke boiled up and waves drifted out, and the sunset that had given wings to Lizzie's memory grew hazy and dull. Sporadic shots punctuated the ominous wail of the police units. Charred fragments of paper floated down and came to rest in the yard. The two women went out to examine the bits of paper.

"Somebody's dream gone up in smoke . . . I wonder how long they waited to get the things that are turning into ashes now." Lizzie's voice was sad.

Sally urged her mother toward the house, went in, and closed the door. Scottie and Richarde came up from the recreation room.

"That sounded like shooting!" exclaimed Richarde.

"That IS somebody shooting . . . ooooooh, look at all that smoke! Come on, let's go see where the fire is!" Scottie was on his way out when Sally blocked the doorway.

"You're not going anywhere — this is a RIOT!"

"A real riot?" he asked in a voice that showed he knew what an awesome thing a riot was.

"Here's a news bulletin!" shouted Richarde, who had raced to the sunroom where the television was.

It was first a "disturbance," later it was a "misunderstanding," and finally, when the reporters had assembled their news and the photographers had developed their pictures, it was a "civil disorder" and Detroit was declared in a state of emergency.

They watched television until all of them were exhausted. The reunion had been enough, but the fear generated by this uncontrolled fighting, looting, and burning drained them. The food, dishes, and kitchen were left untouched as they dragged themselves to bed.

Sally set up a card table and they ate breakfast in front of the television, listening to the debate on who had the authority to call out the National Guard. Once it was decided, they watched a enormous jet screech to a halt and hundreds of battle-geared young men disembark.

A curfew was announced. Later that evening, jeeps loaded with National Guardsmen with guns cradled in their arms paraded down the quiet street, stern-faced and ready for action.

Lizzie came in and sat down to watch as the news reports showed the devastation of the city.

"How senseless . . . it's the time we live in," she said.

The report continued as all programs were preempted. The wounded were taken to hospitals. The number of dead rose higher. Fire equipment, police units, and ambulances filled the city with a mournful, symphonic dread.

"That's all that's left." A woman was weeping and pointing to the pillars standing gaunt against the smouldering ruins of what had been her home. The picture switched to a block of blazing buildings, then gave a close-up of the frustrated firemen standing helplessly by.

Lizzie's eyes filled with tears. Her mind went back, flicking time like the wind-blown pages of a magazine. She stood gazing up at the stars that clustered the Alabama sky on the threshhold of her own dream. . . .

Sometime after midnight, Lizzie grew weary and struggled out of her chair, still thinking about the charred paper falling on the lawn so near the home she cherished.

"If this earthly tabernacle is dissolved, I have another building . . . not made with hands," she said to no one in particular and started up the stairs, humming John's favorite hymn: "On Jordan's stormy banks I stand. . . ."

185

BIBLIOGRAPHY & NOTES

Condon, Mable Green. 1962. HISTORY OF HARLAN COUNTY (Parthenon Press).

. . . When the early scouts came into this section there was only a blazed trail from the western part of Virginia to this area. Many of the early families walked most of the way, bringing only what they could carry because the road would not accommodate a team of oxen . . . . (p. 29).

Daines, Marvel. 1940. BE IT EVER SO TUMBLED, pp. 28, 49 (Citizens Housing & Planning Council of Detroit Research Report).

The *Detroit Free Press*, 10/15/47 (Vol. 117, No. 164, p. 9). "High Court Sets Aside Land Ruling".

Lansing—The Supreme Court upset a Recorder's Court verdict that would have deprived 22 Negro families of their homes and used the land for recreational purposes.
In a seven to one decision with Justice Neil E. Reed dissenting, the Court held that the condemnation jury should have been given all of the facts.
The Court declared that the lower tribunal had erred in refusing to let the jury consider that the City owned a 26-acre plot one block from the condemned property bounded by Wisconsin, Cherrylawn, Chippewa and Norfolk. . . .

Kincaid, Robert. 1955. THE WILDERNESS ROAD (Bobbs Publishing Co.: Indianapolis).

. . . The prevailing homes were single room cabins built of logs chinked and daubed like the crude structures put up by the first settlers. . . . They were straight, slim, with angular features unanimated but intelligent. The men were fierce and crafty; the women listless and sad. A depressive melancholy pervaded every home. They were little interested in the outside world . . . . (p. 306).

Middleton, Elmon. 1934. HARLAN COUNTY, KENTUCKY (Adams Publishing).

. . . Nolansburg, located in Harland County could be reached by railroad. The Louisville & Nashville Railroad was finally induced to extend its railroad into Harlan County, which extension was accomplished in 1910. This marked the beginning of a rapid development of one of the leading coal fields in the United States. In 1911 the Wallins Creek Colliers Company opened the first mines in Harlan County . . . . (p. 53).

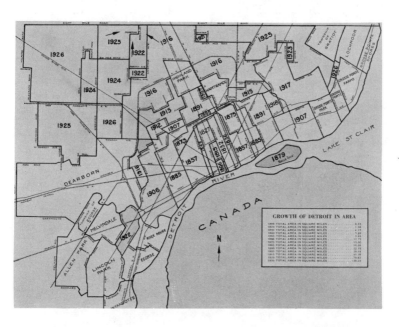

Fig. 1. Growth of Detroit by Annexation (as of 1926).

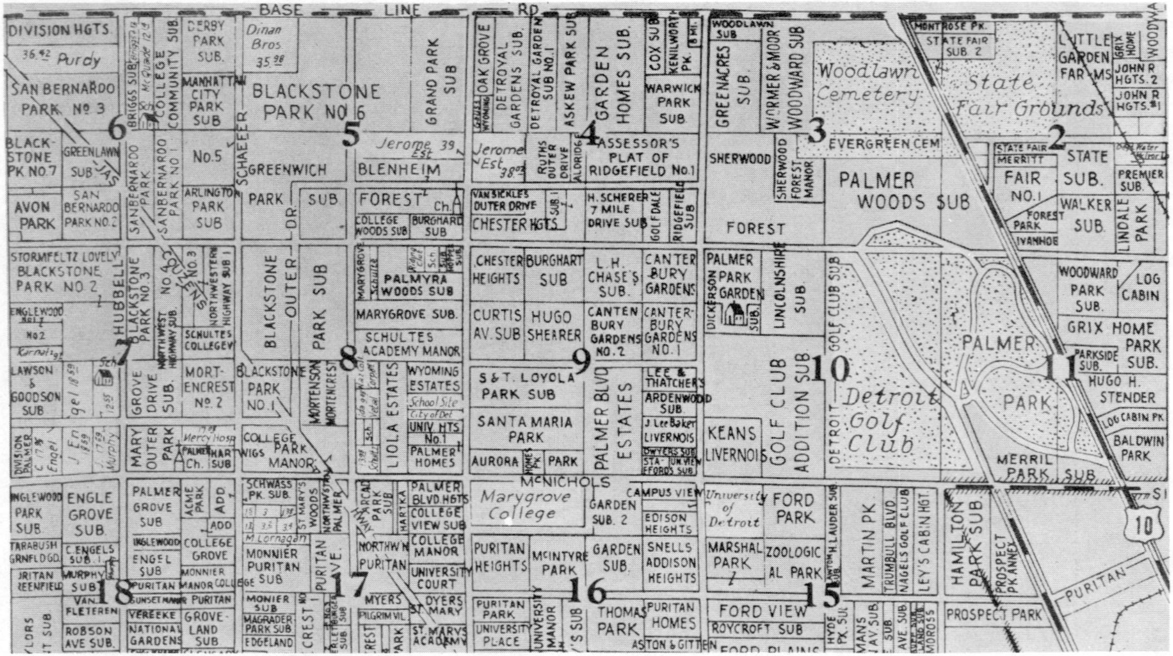

Fig. 2. Part of Northwest Detroit (1921)

188

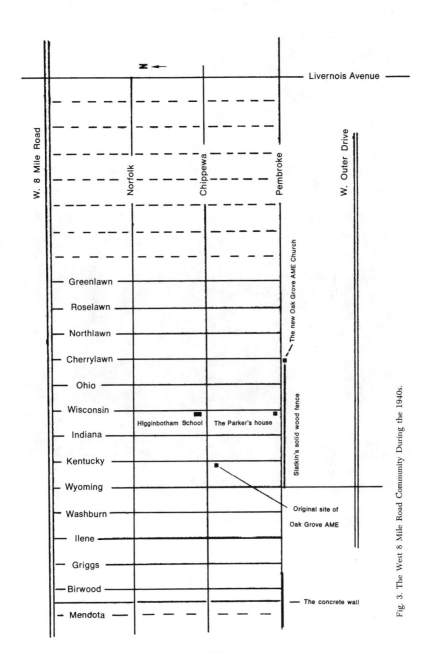

Fig. 3. The West 8 Mile Road Community During the 1940s.

Fig. 4. A portion of the concrete wall from Pembroke north to W. 8 Mile Road erected at the alley on the lots that face Mendota Ave.

Fig. 5. A part of Slatkin's solid wood fence extending eastward along Pembroke from Wyoming to Cherrylawn Avenues, and then south to St. Martins.

INDEX

ABOUT THE AUTHOR —

In this, her first book, Burniece Avery tells the story of her own family starting around 1911 in York, Ala. and their experiences over the next 56 years through Va., Ohio, Ky., and finally Detroit. While this is her first book, it is by no means her first experience in the literary world for theater goers know her best as a playwright and director and as a distinguished actress of stage and television. Her most recent stage performance was in Lillian Hellman's *The Little Foxes* where she played the lead role of Addie in the Meadow Brook Theatre's 1976 season. On the same stage two years earlier, she starred as Berenice Sadie Brown in *Member of the Wedding.* Away from the Meadow Brook Theatre she appeared in *The Miracle Worker* at the Actor's Theater in Louisville, and at other theaters as Miss Judson in *Purlie Victorius;* as Mrs. Venable in *Suddenly Last Summer;* as Mrs. Younger in *A Raisin in the Sun;* and as Grace Kumalo in *Lost in the Stars.* She has also appeared in *Sorry, Wrong Number; Green Pastures; Fisherman and His Wife; Ghost Sonata;* and *Oedipus.* For two seasons she toured with the Milan Company and Linmar Productions and was the leading actress in *Langston Hughes Looks at Dark America.* Her television credits include appearances on "Juvenile Court", "Traffic Court", "Black and Unknown Bards", and *A Raisin in the Sun* for public television in Detroit, WDET. She was the leading actress in "CPT", an hour-long dramatic series for 13 weeks on public television. As a playwright and director, Burniece Avery's *Death Rehearsal* competed in a theatre festival at the Detroit Institute of Arts in 1971, and her television drama in three acts, "Smouldering", was screened six times in 1971 on public television in the Detroit area. She has other written and produced works to her credit and is currently a member of the Detroit Women Writers. From February to November, 1975, she served as talent coordinator for the nation's only black-owned television station (Channel 62 in Detroit) until the soap opera was postponed indefinitely. Lastly, Burniece Avery taught in the Detroit Public school system from 1953 to 1973 with a two-year leave of absence for a theatre tour during this time.